DEDICATION

To everybody who has ever felt lonely and struggled to be herself/himself.

CONTENTS

ACKNOWLEDGMENTS

My parents, Igor Muratov and Olga Muratova, I thank you enormously for giving me the best opportunities in my life you could give. Your love is always with me.

My husband, Ivan Yevseyev, without your support I couldn't accomplish this book! You always believe in me much more than I do. You are the best partner I could wish for.

My friend, Tim Doherty, you encouraged me to finish this book in 2019. Without you I would most likely postpone my writing for a few years.

My friend, Mike Wignall, thank you for your emotional support and for promotion of my book!

My mentor, Kelly Falardeau, without your guidance and feedback I would struggle a lot with writing and publishing my book. Thank you for being flexible in working with me.

My counsellor, Tatiana Antonova, I thank you so much for being with me during difficult times and for helping me to become myself.

.

Part One

The Story

CHAPTER 1
LONELINESS

Being two years old, I was standing in a room full of other kids, but my vision was fixed squarely on the window. Past the stained glass surrounded by a wooden frame covered by cracked white paint, I was watching my mom leave. For the first time, I felt a sense that at the time, could only be described as horrific... a feeling of being abandoned, followed by profound loneliness. I was left all alone in a room with a bunch of strangers. Where was mom going? Why did she leave me behind? I was overcome by terror, and inside I heard a whisper: "She is never coming back."

This was the beginning of my nursery school life. The day went by slowly as if it was reluctant to leave but finally, evening came, and my mother did come back. However, my relief didn't last long. The next day, I was left there again. For consequent five years at nursery and preschool, which also provided daycare for kids, I hated being there.

Nursery school and preschool were located in the same building, and each class had its own rooms where kids slept at day time, played, ate and learned. That two-story grey brick building was near the apartment building where I lived with my parents. One of the rooms occupied by preschool was facing my apartment building. I remember myself around six years old, standing at that room near the window and looking at the apartments. I immensely wanted to go home. Seeing my home and not being able to go there hurt me enormously.

"Why do I have to be here?" – I shouted inwardly. I could do nothing to escape; I felt helpless and powerless.

Painful memories of nursery and preschool are forever imprinted in my mind. During those years, I came to realize the pain of being alone and helpless. These feelings that I would face many times later in life.

I was born in USSR in 1986. My parents lived in Kirovsk, a small town in the north of Russia. This place is located above the arctic circle and has a very harsh living condition. For example, you barely see the sun there during winter because of the polar night. The summer is very bright but cold and short. As a child, I didn't feel the effects of that hard climate on me. I enjoyed spending a lot of time outdoors with my friends. We climbed huge piles of snow, built snow forts, and slid on the hills.

In December of 1991, the Soviet Union collapsed that changed the lives of many people. The dissolution of the USSR was abruptly followed by an economic crash affecting the whole country. My parents were busy surviving – making only enough money to get by. They worked as sports coaches; mom specialized in figure skating and dad in downhill skiing. Job wages were paid out from the municipal budgets and given the challenging political situation wages were often delayed for months at a time. There was often no money. However, if my parents had money, there were no groceries to buy at the store. All the shelves were empty.

My parents lost any real bearings on how to function in the

newly-collapsed economy. The Soviet Union as a political structure was already deep underwater, but nothing new had yet emerged. The sense of stability disappeared since having a job no longer guaranteed a stable wage. It was also dangerous to open your own company because of gangs that sprung up in the area. Business was commonly associated with criminals, and my parents felt stuck. Sometimes, my mom would cry on her way home from work. She was devastated by the inability to cook dinner because there was no food at home.

The government launched a program– grocery coupons strictly rationed out to families in proportion to how many children they had. Grocery coupons were somewhat helpful. To use them, we would go to a particular grocery store called "Chamomile," where we could trade coupons for food. After feeling totally bored, waiting in a long line and for a long time, we were finally able to get an insufficient amount of strict-necessity products. Each individual on the long lineup usually wondered aimlessly about their personal thoughts, but almost everyone was united by a sour look expecting a very bland dinner. As for me, I didn't think about dinner because my little mind was too preoccupied, thinking about the name of the store. The thing was that I could never understand why the store was called "Chamomile", a beautiful delicate flower, and the store was so decrepit, barren and visually unsettling. I never cracked the logic of those adults that decided to give a very ugly store the name of such a beautiful object.

Like a ship that got caught up in a storm, my family did everything it could not to crash in shallow water or hit an underwater reef. For example, in the fall, we collected mushrooms to augment our monotonous food regimen. We weren't the only ones. You often see other mushroom pickers in the good parts of the forest. I remember when we went to visit other families, one of them had mushroom soup, and another family offered fried potatoes with mushrooms. Mushrooms effectively replaced meat and could be served in any form: cooked, salted, dried, and boiled.

In the summer, we visited my grandparents. My paternal grandparents lived in the village in the central part of Russia. This village is called Motmos and located 500 km to the east of Moscow. Each summer, we traveled 2000 km by train to get there. My grandparents grew vegetables, herbs and berries in their garden. After 1-1,5 months, it was time to leave; my parents packed our bags with as much food as they could. Then we carried heavy bags to my native town Kirovsk. To cover the distance in 2000 km, we needed to take buses, a few long-distance trains, and have a transit stop in Moscow. My sister and I were responsible for our small bags filled not only with our toys but also with zucchini, cucumbers and other food items.

My maternal grandparents spent half of the year in the old village Shuya which is located in Karelia (part of Russia to the north of Saint-Petersburg). We stopped there on our way back to Kirovsk from Motmos, expanding our provision. Each summer, we collected small leaves and flowers of willowherb. We wore several layers of clothing to protect ourselves from mosquitoes as we walked around the fields amongst tall plants. When we came home, I helped put leaves and flowers of the herb through the meat grinder and get them ready for drying. This way we prepared tea reserves for the whole winter.

The early nineties were a hard time for many people in Russia. Personally, it's hard to imagine how much inner strength my parents had to keep for withstanding such pressure. In addition to finding new ways to obtain food, they learned to sew. Dad made clothes for skiing and everyday life. My mom created different dresses for me and my sister to wear at kids' parties and at the gatherings at preschool and elementary school. Even though my parents didn't have enough money during the nineties, they always put aside the necessary amount for skiing equipment and English lessons for me and my sister.

Life was extremely stressful, and a lot was going on in our family at that time. Dad used alcohol to eliminate or downplay stress. It was heartbreaking for me to see him drunk and no longer acting like himself. Dad's drinking, the uncertainty and the feeling of helplessness created strong discord in our home. Sometimes my parents argued. When they did, I felt terrified and hoped they would be normal again. I naively believed that if I showed up while they were fighting, it would make them stop. Often times, when I was lying in bed in the evening, I heard their voices getting louder. Tension gripped me from head to toe.

As I am lying in bed, I use every cell in my body to try to make out the piercing words coming out of the kitchen. I am only nine years old and the only one capable of defending my mom and little sister from their tears because of my dad's aggression. My parent's voices are getting louder and louder, and I could not wait any longer. I am shaking inside, but I leave my bed, grip the cold metal door handle and slowly open the door. I see my parents having an argument in the kitchen. I notice the anger on my dad's face and tension rises inside me. I look at my mom; she is cowering and scared but the yelling continues to escalate.

I freeze for a moment while deciding if the situation is critical. No, it is distressing but not awful. The water trick should work. I walk into the kitchen towards the sink, pour myself a glass of water and drink it slowly. I try to spend as much time in the kitchen as possible, hoping that my appearance will calm down the situation. Finally, I take the last sip and walk back to the bedroom where my little sister is sleeping.

We like sleeping on the same bed. I hug my sister and at the same time, I realize that my trick didn't work and my parents are still fighting. I keep listening as I get ready for the next action. Crying and asking them to stop usually works better, but that's for critical situations only. Tonight, the voices seem to be getting quieter and listening intensely; I finally fall asleep.

A few times in my childhood, I had to leave my bed in the

middle of the night together with my mother and sister and stay at the neighbor's apartment. We walked away because dad was acting aggressively. I was petrified by the situation. However, days after the argument was even worse because my parents didn't talk to each other. After the fight, the apartment felt like a high voltage field, and you had to be very careful to avoid getting shocked by the wrong word or action. All I could really think about at that time was how soon this was going to end. When would I see smiles back on the faces of my dear parents again?

Another challenge at the time was seeing my dad drunk outside the house, out in the open, he could be seen by others. It felt like real torture for me: feeling embarrassed, feeling guilty, and just wanting to hideaway. Sometimes it got so bad I literally wished I could sink through the ground and disappear! I hated him at those moments.

However, my love for my dad was always stronger than the hate I felt. I would help my dad get home when he was drunk. Sometimes I just wanted to leave him there and walk away, but of course, I couldn't do that. I loved him so much! Instead, I held him up when he tripped, helped him get up when he fell and answered his drunk questions. I hid my sense of shame and anger which bubbled up inside me.

I felt powerless in solving dad's alcoholic problem. I fantasized that dad would get sick with some dangerous disease which would make him choose: alcohol or his life. When I graduated from high school, everything played out exactly as I dreamed in childhood. My dad actually did get sick. Accidentally, during blood donation, a disease was found in his body. It is hard to communicate just how guilty I felt remembering my childish fantasies.

"This is horrible!!! Is this really my fault? How in the world could I wish something like this on my father?" I tried to keep calm and stay out of my head, but it was unreal.

Luckily medication helped, and he got better. I think it wasn't just good medicine that saved him; it was his own choice. He chose to live; he stopped drinking!

In a later conversation with my mom, I found out that she also secretly hoped he would get sick and quit drinking. She blamed herself when he got ill in the same way I did. In reality, I wasn't alone with that guilt feeling. However, the lack of communication with my mom took away the needed understanding and support.

I understand that my parents put everything they could into keeping the family afloat and to provide for my sister and me better living conditions. Nevertheless, something was missing, something significant to me that they just had no energy or resources for at that time. Years ago, in their childhood, there were even more harsh moments, and their parents were equally engrossed in surviving. This left my grandparents distant from their children emotionally. My parents, who struggled with acceptance and expressing their emotions just didn't know how to be emotionally intimate with themselves and also with us the children. True intimacy was unlikely to happen. The feeling I missed most at that time was a sense of closeness to my parents. I often felt lonely.

Intimacy cannot happen without an emotional connection. My parents were always in the sense of high alert and worry; it was impossible for them to be in contact with me and to 'contain' my feelings. They couldn't adequately provide a safe 'container' for my negative and scary feelings, and act as a safe space between me and the world at large. My parents were full up to the neck with tension and anxiety, and there was just no more space to take on my worries without being pushed underwater. I was left on my own with my distress and fears which were just too much to process without support. What could I do? I suppressed them and moved away from the damaging emotions and worries. I pushed them down inside, deeper and deeper. It only exacerbated the feeling of loneliness. At the time, it became difficult to share with my parents what I really felt, whether good or bad.

Luckily, there were two more members of our family which gave me the much-needed support and lessened my feeling of loneliness. The first family member was my little sister. How lucky I was! Having only four years difference in age, we spent a lot of time together. I am very grateful to my parents for the gift of having another person so close to me and the joy that came with it. She was born at the end of spring when I was 2000 km away in a village, where my paternal grandparents lived. I went to visit them every summer. I remember when grandma and I went to our relatives that had a stationary phone. Grandmother called my dad and let me talk to him.

"You have a sister!" I heard a familiar voice on the other end of the line.

I was overwhelmed by an incredible cocktail of feelings. Tears came to my eyes and dripped down my little cheeks.

"How can I stay here in the village when my sister was just born?" I thought and felt a strong desire to see her. Tears weren't dripping anymore but rolled down my face like little rivers.

"I want to go! Drive me back so I can see her!" I demanded from my grandma.

I adored my sister from the first time I saw her. She was sleeping in her little crib; she was so small with tiny fingers on her hands. I hope I was a fantastic older sister. I took care of her the best way I could. I always tried to be close to her. When she was barely over a year old, I learned to put her to sleep in the crib. I was only five years old myself and couldn't reach her bed like adults, so I devised a new system. I walked to a large armchair that stood next to the crib, climbed up on it myself, and then pulled up my sister. Then I climbed into the crib and asked my sister to crawl closer which allowed me to pick her up and put her down in the crib. Grown-ups were in disbelief that this was even possible and was delighted to see me do it.

Later on, my sister joined me in a daycare but, of course, ended up in a younger group of kids. I was around seven years old, so I was in the oldest class of pre-school. One time there were some technical issues in our room, and we had to vacate.

Our class was split up and temporarily joined to a few younger classes.

Shortly after a teacher was reading us a fairy-tale. When she finished, she wondered why I hadn't asked to join my sister's class.

"And really…why didn't I?" I thought, taking her words very seriously.

The next day I refused to go to preschool to my temporary class. I wanted to be with my sister, and I didn't care if her class was full of little kids that would be 'boring to play with' as adults claimed. I spent the remaining years of my pre-school in the youngest group with my sister. I only left for daytime sleep because the younger class' space didn't have beds that were long enough for me.

Starting at the beginning of elementary school, it became my responsibility to pick up my sister from nursery school and then from preschool, since my parents worked in the evenings. By then, the nursery school and preschool I went to closed down, and my sister attended a new one farther away. There was a day a new preschool teacher refused to let me pick up my sister, saying I was too little. I remember how I cried on my way back to our neighbors, dragging an empty sleigh behind. Because my parents were at work, we stayed with our neighbours while waiting for our mom and dad to come back home. The neighbors were an older couple whom we really liked, but for some reason, my complaints were met without empathy at that time. The neighbor said I should have insisted and picked up my sister anyway. I went back to my sister's preschool being terrified of getting another refusal. Luckily, another teacher recognized me. I picked up my sister, put her on a sleigh and slid her back home with a big smile on my face.

When my sister got a little older, we started to enjoy playing together. We were teachers, doctors, librarians, but most of all, we loved to play mother-daughter. Using chairs, blankets and other objects we made a makeshift house right in the middle of our room. We filled the house with clothes from the closet, pillows from the bed and kitchen pots and pans from the kitchen. The center of the house was taken up by a standing lamp. It was always a little crowded inside, but it had a unique sense of coziness and comfort. For a time, I became the little daughter, and my sister took the role of a caring mother. Probably, during those moments, I was filled up with the care that I didn't get enough from the relationship with my parents. Kids are amazing natural psychologists and use play to get over traumatic experiences and negative emotions. My sister and I, using games to play, gave each other support that helped us get through emotionally tough times.

Another family member which was one foot tall was my dog. My parents bought her just before my sister was born. I was three years old. A straw-colored Cocker Spaniel called Motya had been living with us for thirteen years, and all those years she was my very best friend. She lay down at my feet when I was doing homework. She slept with me in my bed and guarded me on my way to a training session and back. I still see her in my dreams. She was an astounding creature and loved me so much. She accepted me fully for who I was. For thirteen years of her life, she gave me strength and comfort. She was always with me during life's most difficult moments.

Simply being there for each other is a precious gift we can give to somebody. Motya taught me that somebody could be with me even if I was angry, sad, or scared. When others failed, she was with me without expectations and words, just with her love and acceptance. She constantly reminded me that I wasn't lonely.

Being this close was necessary for me because some life events hit me very hard. One of them was my first trip abroad at the age of ten years. I went to compete in downhill competitions in Sweden. Because my native town is located four hours away from the border with Finland, we were getting to Sweden by bus. When we approached Russian customs, we had to exchange buses as Finnish bus drivers were waiting for us there. Growing up in a country with a limited amount of food and things in stores, with lack of municipal services, I was astonished by well-maintained houses, roads and streets. When we stopped for a break, our Finnish drivers bought us food in a cafeteria where for the first time, I ate a pizza.

During the ride, I noticed with surprise the absence of any customs between Finland and Sweden. It seemed so unrealistic that people could cross the border when they wanted and without providing passports. Sweden town at our destination was lovely. We even had a chance to do a little bit of sight-seeing between our training and competitions. For the first time, I could speak English with somebody who wasn't Russian. It was hard but I managed to have small conversations. I was fully satisfied with my first trip when it was time to go back.

However, our way to Russia differed a lot from the first half of our trip. When we stopped for a break, we were already hungry. I expected that we would get some food as we did on our way to Sweden, but it never happened. Our Finish drivers bought food only for themselves. I assume the budget for our dinner wasn't planned by our sports club or somebody else who organized the trip. Fortunately, we had some snacks with us and were able to satisfy our hunger a little bit. Another unpleasant surprise was waiting for us at the Finnish customs. Finnish customs officers refused to let our bus to the Russian border. I don't know what the cause was, but I vividly remember crossing the neutral zone between two borders by feet and carrying my bag and ski bag with me. However, it wasn't the end of our struggles. When we arrived to Russian customs, the officers said that there was no bus for us. Nobody came to take us to my native town. It was late evening, and the officers didn't know what to do with us. We were waiting outdoor because the Russian border only had a few small portable offices. I couldn't get it why nobody came for us and was worried. When both borders were closed, the officers took us to their homes as there was nothing else they could do.

I remember that it was extremely cold in their apartments in a two-story building. Everything looked old and gloomy. I occupied an armchair in the living room and tried to sleep. However, other kids who were older were watching a movie on the TV. It was a horror movie as I hadn't experienced enough stress yet. I was scared by the movie and the whole situation and couldn't fall asleep for a while. In the morning a bus came to take us home.

Another stressful event happened when I was 12 years old. At that time, I reached the pinnacle of my youth downhill skiing career. At the beginning of spring, I won one of the leading national skiing competitions in my age group. The prize was a surprise trip to Italy to compete internationally which was accompanied by the first-ever plane flight, dinner buffet, and icy slalom course.

Since those national skiing competitions were run in my native town Kirovsk, our team, made up of kids from all over Russia, got on the train from Kirovsk to Moscow and then on the plane to Italy. The trip to a small Italian town with ski slopes was lovely and fun, except for getting car sick. After our arrival in Milan, we hopped on a bus and after a short drive, stopped at a buffet restaurant. I'd never experienced such an abundance of food. In the beginning, I couldn't believe that I was allowed to choose whatever I wanted and to eat as much as I could. Being hungry after the flight and overwhelmed by all salads, main dishes and desserts, I overate. Later, when our bus was on the narrow winding roads in the mountains, I became extremely car sick and felt awful. Fortunately, when we arrived at our destination, I started to feel much better right away. We spent at that place approximately five days.

I have a lot of vivid memories from that trip, but one that stands out the most, and feels most horrible, happened on the way back home and has stuck with me to this day. Our team flew back to Moscow, where everyone separated and went back to their hometowns. My trip continued to the north to my native town, from which I was the only one from. The Moscow coach who was our guide and I arrived at the train station in the middle of the capital. The coach said he had some errands to run at home. He left me alone at the station close to the statue of Lenin to watch my luggage. I don't know how long exactly he was gone, but it felt like an eternity. Lack of mobile phones and any follow-up connections made that situation long and hopeless.

Minute ticked after a minute, and I felt more and more disconcerted. I was twelve years old and was in the middle of Moscow alone with no money or connections. Loneliness and unsettling feelings gulped me. I saw crowds of people in front of my eyes, some rushing to make a trip, others killing time by leisurely strolling or studying the outside of the convenience store. Whatever they were doing, they looked busy and were entirely oblivious to my presence. I kept waiting. Soon, I noticed I was hungry because my stomach started to growl; I was facing a convenience store but had no money for food.

All of a sudden, a soldier rushed away from his group and walked over to me. He reached out his hand and gave me a pastry, adding that I looked hungry. I was probably looking at them with such an intense stare; he knew it without saying. I happily accepted the gift. Fortunately, after a long wait, the coach was back. I remember he bought me a bag of orange juice. He may have purchased other stuff for me, but for an unknown reason, the orange juice is all I remember. It was time to get on the train, the coach put me in one of the railcars, and I watched the statue of Lenin, the soldiers, and the convenience store get farther and farther away. What didn't leave me was the sense of loneliness and fear.

The trip from Moscow to Kirovsk took an endless two nights and one day. I occupied the bottom bunk bed and across from me was an elderly man. He was my companion and friend for the ride and eased my state for the lonely trip. Orange juice was not enough to subdue my hunger, but he was kind enough to share food with me. Staring out the window, I dreamed of coming home back to my parents, to my little sister and our room we shared together and leaving the trip in the past. I fantasized about our apartment, which still was the safest place for me despite all the unhappy moments associated with it. I wanted to be surrounded by my things and toys. Disappointment hit me as soon as I was back. I found out we were temporarily living with our relatives because my parents rented out our apartment to tourists who came to ski. My state got even worse by this news. The tension between my parents that I also discovered was another huge concern for me. All the things I dreamed of or imagined on the train didn't happen, and instead, I had to clutch my fists and do everything I could to reduce conflict between my parents.

I didn't say a word about my trip, my sense of fear and loneliness. I told my parents about that trip and how I felt almost twenty years later. Before working with a counsellor, I didn't even realize I hid from them such critical information. During one of the sessions with a counsellor, I saw that I held this to myself for all these years, and I felt amazed by this discovery! For a while, I couldn't even understand why I did it. It made sense that a child going through a hard time would share it with their parents. That's how I feel now, but back then, I thought just about everyone else needed help but not me. I thought the grown-ups were the ones who required support; I was too independent to ask for help.

Thanks to happy moments in my childhood, I was able to sustain my negative experiences. Camping during the summer holiday was one of these inspiring, joyful moments. During every visit to my maternal grandparents in Shuya village, we took off on a small adventure. We went camping on a small island in the White Sea. The cold bleak sea in the north of Russia created so many warm memories for me.

On the day before the trip, we prepared the necessary equipment, tools and food. My dad carefully calculated high and low tides so we could safely reach the island. Everybody had some tasks to accomplish and I was proud to help my dad in the preparation.

The next day during high tide, we put everything in the white boat with a motor at the back. The boat had a pretty flat bottom and was wide. Everybody in the family called that boat

– "soap-dish." After taking our seats, we slowly went down the river which ran across the village. I usually stayed in front of the boat, so I could navigate the boat's movement by pointing any underwater stones to my dad who was rowing. The motor could be used only at the end of the village, where lesser hidden obstacles in the water were located.

It took maybe 10-15 minutes to get to that start point. Then my dad moved close to an old motor. To start the engine, he used the special rope, which he reeled up around one of the details under the motor cover and then quickly pulled the rope. We expected to hear sounds of the motor when my dad had twitched the end of the rope. But there was only silence. Dad did the same procedure the second time. Again, we heard nothing. Everybody became worried and was staring at the rope in dad's hands. He slowly reeled it around the detail.

"I want to camp so much! Please, please, start-up!" I thought with hope and listened attentively.

"Grrrr" The motor started to rumble. I smiled and turned forward. Cool wind touched my face. I hugged my dear dog that was sitting close to me, and my heart was filled with happiness.

The river flowed into the White sea after five kilometers. We passed many tiny islands on the way to our favorite one. Finally, after a few hours, we reached the rocky shore of the island. Nobody was there and I felt it was our land. After helping adults to move everything from the boat and unpacked our stuff, my sister and I ran to explore our territory.

The island was covered by different trees with the shore composed of huge rock layers. Those flat slightly inclined rocks stretched to the water. The surf polished the stones, making them very convenient to walk on. My sister and I slowly went away from the camping spot. The low tide had begun, and we could see small puddles on the rocks. We bent over one of the puddles and observed its tiny inhabitants for a while. Then we decided to go around the island. During that walk, we became brave mariners who explored discovered lands. Our path led through stone obstacles, logs thrown into the shore, and fallen trees. During breaks, we sat on a soft reindeer moss that covered stones close to the forest and ate huckleberries. Berries grew on small bushes and were extremely tasty.

After exploration of the island, we came back to the camp, tired, happy, and with faces and hands coloured by huckleberries. Adults had already cooked lunch. My sister and I shared with adults our stories about the expedition and then found "table" and "chairs" among big stones close to the camp. After taking our plates, we went to our improvised dining room and started to eat soup with huge appetites. The soup was the most delicious meal I ever had! It was made from simple ingredients such as potatoes, canned meat, mushrooms that were found on the island, small noodles, and dried veggies. Nothing special, but the time spent outdoors, the unusual setting and the excitement, all these made that soup the best dish in the world!

While we had our long walk around the island and the lunch, low tide reached its peak and created new areas for exploration. During the low tide level, the sea decreased for two meters, leaving many meters of sea bottom uncovered. There are no so many sea creatures in the north seas as in the warm seas. However, we walked on that sandy open space with high interest. In addition, because of the constant wind, that open space had big benefit - fewer mosquitoes than places close to the trees.

In the evening, covered by many layers of clothes for protection from mosquitos, we sat around an organized fireplace and talked. The night in the camping tents was part of the adventure. In the morning, after having breakfast, we went to pick huckleberries. At home, we would make a jam from those tasty berries to enjoy during the winter months. I always liked to pick berries with my mom. Nobody was in a rush, and we talked about various topics. For example, I asked her about her and my father's first meeting, about her years at the University in Saint-Petersburg, and about myself as a little baby. I also liked to share with her something from my life and my thoughts and ideas. All these made us closer, and thus made me extremely happy!

Usually, we spent two days and one night on the island, and then went back to the village. Every time it was sad to leave that adventure behind. However, we had many interesting things to do in the village too. For instance, during one of the summers, my sister and I did a little bit of fishing at the river.

Firstly, it was necessary to get worms. We found them under narrow wooden planks that were on the ground. These small light planks laid on the path and served as small bridges in rainy weather. My sister and I collected the necessary amount of bait without problems. Then we went down to the river and took our fishing spots on the closest to water big stones. We cast long fishing rods that were too big for us and waited. The catch was tiny, but we proudly went home and fed our cats with these small fish.

We loved to stay near the river, which had high and low tides. That is why we needed to calculate the proper time for our fun on the water. During the low tide, we could explore long lines of stones. My sister and I often walked on them, carefully stepping from one big stone to another. One of those lines was so long that it almost reached an opposite bank of the river.

During the high tide, we went swimming in the river. To get to a small pier, we had to be cautious, going down on the wooden stairs. Some of the steps were old and unstable. In some places, there were high chances to be stung by nettles. The water wasn't very warm, but we didn't care. After spending a lot of time in the water, we came home with blue lips and drank hot tea.

When I was about eleven years old, I went to the river with a few of my friends. That day we decided to swim along the large fishing boat anchored close to the bank. One anchor was dropped from the front of the boat, and another from the stern. At first, we swam to the anchor rope, which was attached to the stern. After a few minutes, we began to swim along the boat one by one. We had to swim against the current. I was confident in my abilities. However, suddenly the water began to pull me under the boat. My heart beat fast! I struggled to keep my head above the water. The power of the water was sinking me under the surface. Horror gripped me. Dimly hearing the frightened screams of the guys: "Stronger strokes! Come on!", I put the last efforts to escape from that whirlpool. Finally, the water let me go, and I swam to the anchor rope in front of the boat and clung to it with trembling hands.

Gradually, my breath became calmer, pulse came back to normal and I was able to get to the pier. I was scared, I couldn't believe that I was so close to being drowned. With depressed feelings, I came home but stayed silent about the accident. To that time, the thought of sharing my feelings and worries with my parents already was alien to me. I coped with that terrible experience all by myself.

My sister and I also liked to visit my grandfather's cousins, who were originally from that village. After moving away to the town, every summer they returned to their native land. They still had a house on the opposite side of the river. We went to them for a cup of tea each time crossing the wooden bridge that connected two banks. Some parts of this bridge were covered with wooden planks. There were uncovered logs in the remaining parts. Of course, my sister and I walked not along the pedestrian path that was formed by planks. We stepped over the logs because it was fun and interesting. Walking there, we looked at the water that was visible through the gaps between the logs.

When we reached the house of my grandfather's cousins, they greeted us hospitably, and we sat on a wooden bench near the table in the kitchen. Jam, candies and cookies in nice glass dishes quickly appeared on the table. Then beautiful elegant cups with saucers were placed in front of us. Two lovely ladies started asking us many questions about our day, and we happily told various stories to those attentive listeners. After some time, the kettle boiled the water. We watched how carefully one of the ladies poured tea for me and my sister. I took a beautiful little cup and poured some amount of tea in a saucer. Then I slowly brought the saucer closer to my face, blew gently on the tea, and finally made a few pleasant sips. This unique tea ritual always brought great pleasure to me. It was something special that I shared only with my sister and those two distant relatives.

I, my sister and my parents went through many different hard situations. Fortunately, our family was able to survive. With time, we learned how to be emotionally closer to each other, and our communication became better. I remember how the process of family rapprochement started. I was around high school age when I suddenly had a burning desire to hug my mom or put my head on her knees when she was sitting on the sofa. It seemed a little awkward, but I decided to go ahead with this physical act. I felt a colossal weight drop off my shoulders. There were many evenings since that when we spent time together, feeling genuine love and connection with each other. I am infinitely grateful to my parents that they kept the family whole. They always were the best parents for me, even though they did make mistakes and weren't ideal parents. But I've never wanted to have a perfect mother and farther; I always wanted to have my mom and my dad. I did, do and will always love them with all my heart.

CHAPTER 2
IN SEARCHING FOR LOVE

When I was a girl and dreaming about my future, I imagined myself with a great husband. I pictured him as a caring, kind, and handsome man. I was sure that I would constantly experience happiness and joy from being with him. Of course, he would understand all my desires and accept me. He would help me to solve all my problems and would always be there for me.

Reality hit me strongly. When I became a teenager and started paying attention to guys, my relationship with them was far away from that childish dream. I didn't give guys an opportunity to care about me. At any convenient situation, I demonstrated how strong and independent I was. At the same time, I thought only about my boyfriend's happiness and disregarded my own feelings and needs. I kept silent about my desires. To my surprise, guys could not read my thoughts and didn't realize my wishes. Instead of happiness and joy, I was immersed in sadness, dissatisfaction and constant fear of losing that relationship. I felt completely stuck in that unhealthy pattern of relationship which I iterated with every guy, it doesn't matter if he was my boyfriend or just a friend.

My childish dream couldn't become a reality. It took me

years to understand why it was an unreal dream. One of the reasons is that in that fantasy, I projected to the imaginary husband qualities I missed in my dad. I also unconsciously summit the ideal relationship I wanted to have with my dad. Of course, it was impossible for any partner to satisfy those bottomless needs of my inner child. Another reason is that I needed to change myself for being able to form a relationship I desired to have with a partner. Staying the same, I couldn't step into healthy interaction with any man.

That unhealthy pattern was extremely strong. It was formed in childhood through communication with my father and became part of my being. My relationship with my dad had a hard start. He was in the army when I was born. The first time he saw me not in the picture but in reality was when I turned nine months old. At that age, I had a difficult time being carried by anybody who wasn't my mom. I resisted being taking in hands by somebody else. My mom was surprised and delighted to see that I stretched my arms towards my dad when he arrived home from the army.

I remember that black and white photo in my parents' photo archive. My dad is in the military uniform, with me standing on his lap, supported by his hands. There is nothing else in the photo except the both of us. My dad looks so handsome and young. He is only twenty-three years old at that time.

Being a coach, my dad wanted to train me. I started to ski when I was three years old. Unfortunately, my dad couldn't separate the two roles of being a father and a coach. He was more of my coach than my dad. Of course, it immensely affected our relationship. To be accepted and loved by him, I had to take the first places and be a strong person. He couldn't bear me crying or being scared, and suppressed my weakness.

My dad wanted the best for me; however, his view on my upbringing was in some ways very different from what I needed. Unfortunately, I don't recall the time we played together. We interacted mostly during training sessions or when we did something useful together. For example, we went together to a garage that was located ten minutes away from our apartment. I helped my dad to clean a driveway from snow. At those moments, I could feel some connection with him. He taught me how to cook tasty pancakes, chop wood, row, paint walls and so on. Every time I cook pancakes or do something else that he taught me, I think about him with love.

I was a sensitive girl, but my dad expected me to be strong, compete with guys and hide my feminine weakness. What I missed was his unconditional attention and acceptance of me as a girl. I wanted him to show genuine attention not only to my sports results but to my feelings, interests and my life. It never happened. I'm filled with sadness in my heart anytime I realize that we can't completely make up for something that was absent in my childhood, such as carefree time together and sincere conversations.

My dad's problems with alcohol made the situation even worse. I never knew what to expect at home. Uncertainty made me very vigilant. It seemed like I constantly scanned space and was ready to react. I learned to read the feelings of others and care about their needs. My parents' happiness was a chance for me to be happy too. Emotional safety wasn't granted to me. I had to earn safety and some sort of stability by shifting focus from myself to others. I became co-dependent and my well-being became dependent on other people. Later in life with all my romantic partners, I built unhealthy co-dependent relationships.

In addition, for many years, I had seen the world as white and black. I couldn't realize that it was possible to stay in a relationship while experiencing polar feelings such as love and hate. In my childhood, certain actions of my dad led to my anger, a lot of which I suppressed and never showed up. At the time, I felt that if I was angry at him, it meant that I hated him. Experiencing those fused feelings, I didn't want him to be in my life at some moments. Then I felt such strong guilt which made me afraid he would leave me forever. In my childhood, I was unable to understand that it was normal to experience different feelings at the same time towards somebody. In my mind, hate and love, anger and love could not coexist; like oil in the water, the two emotions just couldn't mix. I felt stuck and unable to escape from that conflict and unbearable emotions.

But how could I have a different attitude to relationships if I had to suppress my anger for staying loved and accepted? My dad could express his irritation and anger. For me, it was forbidden. The pain which I felt from his behavior and lack of unconditional acceptance definitely shaped me and my mindset. Of course, the overall environment also contributed a lot to my views on relationships. In my family and in the families of my grandparents, a man was given more privilege than a woman. For instance, they didn't do most of the house chores, could dictate what to watch on TV, didn't say sorry and didn't care about somebody's personal stuff. My mother and my grandmothers most of the time didn't stand up for themselves in all range of situations from an unpleasant comment about their clothes to big conflicts. I believed that a man was more important than a woman. I was afraid to show my irritation and anger which led to problems with the protection of my personal boundaries. I felt like someone from a lower class because I was a girl.

My personal experience with different gender was strange. On one hand, I preferred to spend time with guys more than girls. Maybe it was because in my sports club I was surrounded mostly by guys my entire childhood. On another hand, I had extremely painful experiences with them at some point. When we became teenagers, something changed dramatically. The guys who interacted with me in a normal way started to bully and make a mockery of me. What a hard time it was! I couldn't understand what had changed in them.

One day we were going to a competition in another town. In the morning we took all our equipment from the sports club and went to the bus that was waiting for us nearby. I entered the bus and occupied one of the seats. The guys were passing, giggling and laughing at me. Nobody sat close to me. It happened that it was the only free seat when the last boy came in. He looked around trying to find another available sit. After he realized that the only option was to sit close to me, he hesitated for a few moments. I couldn't get what the problem was. When the guy finally occupied that last seat, other guys started laughing at him.

"He is seating with her" They mocked.

I felt that they saw me as something terrible. Nobody wanted to be with me, even to seat close to me was something awful for them. Feeling so ashamed and totally rejected, I tried not to cry. I just wished to get out from there. A few minutes later, a driver started the engine, and our bus began its trip. The guys stopped laughing, but I continued to wonder why they don't like me.

"It is probably because I am a girl," I concluded after some time.

When I was around thirteen-fourteen years old, I went to the training camps during the summer. My team and I spent some time in Belarus and Ukraine working on strength, endurance, agility and other skills. My team included thirteen athletes: twelve boys and myself. During that time, I experienced conflicting feelings. On one hand, I regularly felt rejected. For example, guys didn't want to take me on the team when we played some sports games, such as volleyball. I was so lonesome.

On another hand, there were some positive moments. Once, a guy from my team stood up for me when other guys were laughing at me. Another time, I and two guys who both shared the same name Ivan, went to a picnic. It was a wonderful moment. At first, we bought candies and juice in the country store. Then we went to the bank of the lake that was close to a place we stayed in. We sat on the grass, enjoying the warm sun, nice view, conversation and sweets. For some time, I really experienced happiness and acceptance. I enjoyed their company and they enjoyed mine that was even more important for me. I am not sure if there is any connection between that experience and my husband, but his name is Ivan.

On my way to healthy relationship in marriage I had to change my attitude to men. Being raised in a co-dependent family, I knew only one way of interacting with other people, especially with guys. Even small attention from somebody to whom I could feel even slight sympathy was enough for me. I fell in love right away. Since that moment, my focus shifted to that guy. Probably, what I experienced can be called obsession. I was constantly daydreaming and thinking about this guy when I had a free moment.

Having my attention on someone else helped me to deal with my anxiety. It didn't matter if we had a relationship or I just knew him from somewhere. In any way, when I focused on a guy, I was able to manage my life. I was able to overcome my fears in sport, tolerate unpleasant and painful events, maintain my hope and have a meaning. My anxiety wasn't so intense, and I could fall asleep without troubles because I imagined something romantic and lovely. It seems like my mind demanded to be preoccupied with those sorts of fantasies, so I could avoid thinking of all the pain I stored inside me.

However, there was an opposite side to that obsession. Every time my relationships ended, I fell in such an unbearable despair that I couldn't imagine continuing living. At the moment when the relationships were over or even if I just felt rejected, I burst into sobbing. My life was over too. Nothing could protect me from my anxiety, painful experiences and despair. I was left all alone. Vulnerable and totally broken.

That is why I was so afraid of losing a relationship. I did everything I could to save it. I put many efforts in making a guy happy. Mostly I did it by betraying myself. Without thinking about my needs and feelings, I focused on him. Probably, I was perceived as needy, but I couldn't help it. I could buy an airline ticket and fly to a different city for the weekend, so I could spend a couple of days with my boyfriend. I could leave my studying behind and help him with his research paper. I could do anything I didn't want to do just to make him happy.

However, nothing worked and after some time, our connection broke, leaving me in the dark pit. Although my despair was so strong, it didn't take me a long time to find somebody else after I recovered emotionally.

In addition, I always unconsciously chose a guy with whom I couldn't build a long-lasting relationship. It could be because he was from a different city, or much younger, or much older, or served in the army, or simply had totally different life views and interests from mine. I didn't notice other guys who probably were better for me as if they couldn't be on my radars.

Gradually, the thought that something wasn't right started to come to my mind. I noticed the stable and enjoyable relationships of other people. It became obvious that there was another way to connect with people and partners. Also, I didn't want to suffer anymore. Probably, I reached the point where I simply didn't want to follow that road of dependency, tears, and emotional pain.

I had no idea how, but after that inner shift, I was able to form a little bit better and healthier relationships with the next man in my life and even more positive with the man after the next one. Sometimes, I still experienced strong unpleasant feelings. However, they weren't so intense as before, and I could manage them. In 2013, I went to the training camp in Canada with the Russian Mogul National Team. At that time, we had Canadian coaches who prepared us for the Olympic Games. My team had been staying in Vancouver for ten days before the long camp in Whistler.

After our arrival, my teammates and I went to a shopping mall. My good friend and teammate Regina and I were walking inside the mall, looking for attractive stores and talking to each other in Russian. I noticed one guy in the middle of the aisle. His attention was caught by something.

"Hmm, pretty interesting guy." I thought while we walked pass him. Then I focused again on the conversation with my friend. Suddenly, we heard that somebody was talking to us in Russian. We turned and looked behind; I saw that it was that guy whom we had just passed.

He approached us and initiated a conversation. My friend Regina left us alone shortly after because she wanted to visit one of the stores nearby. At least, she made that excuse, but I suspect she just decided to create a more intimate atmosphere for me and my new acquainted. The name of the guy was Ivan. He was Russian and recently moved to Canada to study. It turned out that some time ago, we lived fifteen minutes' drive from each other in the suburb of Moscow. He is originally from a small town called Kubinka, which is located 40 km east from Moscow. While I was working as a manager of a sport team and some time after, I rented an apartment in another town that was close to Kubinka. I even visited Kubinka a few times because I had a friend there. I wonder if Ivan and I ever passed each other or were on the same suburban electric train at that time. Although we lived so close to each other in Russia, we met in Canada in a shopping mall.

Ivan and I continued talking until Regina returned. Ivan was really nice and interesting to talk to, but it was time to say goodbye.

"It was nice to meet you. See you later." Ivan said before going away.

"Wait a minute! I don't have your contacts. How are we supposed to meet again?" I replied with a little bit of flirting in my voice.

"Yes, of course, here is my Facebook." He found a small piece of paper, wrote down his contact information and handed that note to me.

"See you later." I replied with a smile.

The day went by and in the evening, I contacted him, so he could know my Facebook contact information as well. Ivan invited me to go out with him.

"Why not?" I thought. "He is a nice guy. It will be great to spend some time together."

Maybe for the first time, there was no obsession or

something like that. I understood that I would leave soon; that is why I didn't expect to have a relationship or fall in love with him. This circumstance eased my usual worries about the interaction with a man. I also had no expectations and simply enjoyed spending time with him.

Since our first date, we went out almost every day. After having two training sessions, I came to my place, had a shower and a simple dinner in a hurry. Ivan would knock on the door a few minutes later I had finished my meal, and we usually went for a walk or did something else. My ten days in Vancouver flew by fast. Fortunately, Ivan was able to visit me in Whistler, where my team moved for the next training camp. He even stayed in Whistler for a while to spend more time with me. After one month of dating Ivan, I realized that I didn't want to leave him. However, our training camp was over, and my team had to move to the next location far away from Canada.

I had no idea what was going to happen next between us. We decided to stay in touch by social media and Skype. It was very sad to separate from him because at that point I already liked him so much. He saw me off to the airport. We hugged each other one more time, and I walked away to the departure zone with sadness in my heart.

Being on different continents most of the time, we still managed to call each other by Skype almost every day. For almost seven months, we had long distant relationship, except for two of my visits to Canada. Surprisingly, our connection grew stronger with time, even though we were far away from each other. We met in July 2013. I came to visit him in October for one week and then in December for a few weeks. We got married in April 2014, after nine months of knowing each other.

This relationship was so different from my previous experiences. Probably, without any expectations at the beginning, I was able to enjoy the time together and not to dive into my obsession. Of course, at some moments, I still dealt with intense feelings. But I could tolerate them and react consciously.

In the fall of 2013, a few months after we met, I knew that we needed to see each other. Ivan couldn't go away because he was studying at college. The only option for us to meet was my visit. However, I also had a very tight schedule with short breaks between training camps. At the same time, I had this feeling inside telling me to go even for a short visit. I knew it wasn't a strong feeling of desperation or something else that came to me before and could push me to act irrationally. For example, I could spend a lot of money and energy on a surprise for my boyfriend.

This time I experienced some calm and less intense feelings. If somebody asked me why I knew it was the right decision to visit Ivan, I couldn't explain. I just felt that if I go, something would shift. Following my intuition, I arranged for a flight to Canada. Before buying my tickets, I talked to Ivan, and we agreed to split the cost of my flights. Even this action of paying together was distinct from my previous strategy. In the past, without any doubts, I could pay for an air ticket all by myself. My first visit to Ivan lasted five days.

The next time I came to spend a few weeks in December. We were able be together for Christmas. I also got to know Ivan's parents. The third time I came to Canada was with my wedding dress and shoes one week before our wedding.

Ivan is a unique person. Even the way he asked me to marry him was unusual. I was in Russia, talking by Skype with him. The Olympic Games had already passed, and we were discussing our plans for the near future. We decided that I would move to Canada.

"Yes, it is not a problem for me to come because my visa lasts for another two years." I said to Ivan.

"It is awesome!" he replied with excitement.

"However, I am still worried about all the paperwork. Can I stay in Canada with a visa? Will I be able to work?" was my response.

"Don't worry! You will marry me." Ivan pronounced with his usual tone.

"Oh!!!" I was caught by a complete surprise. Lingering, I

added with alertness in my voice. "Ok. Are you proposing to me?"

"Yes." He reassured me.

"Wow! I am so shocked! It sounds wonderful!" My heart rate was up, and I barely could sit still. My body had an impulse to dance and jump around.

My mother in law and Ivan prepared a small reception in the Vancouver downtown. When we arrived at the restaurant after the photo session, I stayed outdoor while Ivan sorted everything out with guests who were waiting for us. It was April and I was standing in my wedding dress near the restaurant but in some distance, so the guest couldn't see me. Some time passed, but Ivan didn't return to me. I didn't have a cell phone just my wedding bouquet, so I couldn't call Ivan. I don't know how much time I spent standing near the nearby hair salon, but after a while, a lady came out and asked me if everything was Ok. I answered that everything was fine, being very surprised by her question. Only when she left, I realized that it probably seemed weird from her perspective that somebody in a wedding dress was standing on a street of downtown for a long time. Finally, Ivan came out, and our wedding began. My parents attended by Skype, drinking sparkling wine at 4 am in the morning because of the time difference. We had a small lovely wedding. The whole new chapter of my life started that day.

I had never lived with somebody. Of course, I spent a lot of time with my teammates and some time with my roommates at University. However, I never shared an apartment with a partner. Living with Ivan was a totally new experience for me. After some time, I realized that married life evokes so many past experiences. Living with a husband, I relived most of my traumatic events. Not because Ivan did something wrong, but because I was immersed into the close family relationship. In the past, those close family connections created a lot of painful and unbearable feelings. Small details of my married life could easily trigger my intense inner response which most of the time was distressing.

For instance, one time, I accidentally broke a night lamp in our rental apartment. Not a big deal. However, for some time, I was paralyzed by overwhelming sensations. Before having any thoughts, I felt a strong response from my body. All my muscles were tensed, and I was holding my breath. I froze like a deer in the middle of the road in front of an oncoming car. For a moment, I imagined that Ivan would be furious.

Then slowly, my brain started to work. I recognized that my reaction was inapplicable to the current situation. Ivan never said something rude to me and never reacted aggressively. At first, I couldn't get why I had such a strong response for such a trivial event. Then I remembered some of my past experiences as a child. My dad couldn't tolerate my mistakes.

Another example is that I couldn't bear when Ivan suddenly went to sleep without saying something to me. For instance, we were sitting in the leaving room and preoccupied attending to our personal needs. Then Ivan went away from the living room. Thinking he would soon be back, I didn't pay attention to his absence and continued cross-stitch and watch Netflix. After some time, it became obvious that he would not come back. Harsh emotions and body sensations smashed me right after I discovered that he was already asleep. My anxiety and feeling of abandonment were so intense that I couldn't live through the night. Time slowed down dramatically. Neither I was able to focus on my activities anymore or fall asleep. My emotions seemed completely unbearable.

The only thing that helped me was the understanding that these feelings would pass. I knew it from my past experiences. I just needed to go through the night, and the next day I would feel much better. Keeping this in my mind, I was able not to fall into despair completely.

When this situation repeated a few times, I talked to Ivan and explained to him how his actions affect me. I shared in detail what was happening with me at those moments and why it occurred. The thing was that when he went to sleep without saying anything to me, I perceived it as a sudden break of our connection. This situation triggered my unhealed parts, which went into a complete panic. I felt abandoned, rejected and totally alone - the feelings which I faced in my childhood but couldn't live through or let go.

Ivan understood me and agreed to always tell me about going to sleep. In this case, the triggering situation couldn't occur. With time I was able not to feel abandoned even if accidentally a similar situation happened.

There were many situations where I face hard moments during my married years. However, all of them became sources of insights and also opportunities for personal growth. Using the help of my counsellor, I healed my suffering parts and became more resistant to different triggers. Thanks to opened safe discussions with my husband, our relationship became much stronger and authentic than ever before.

For many years I was searching for love. I thought that somebody could make me feel loved and accepted. A partner represented to me a provider of everything I was missing. After searching for love in another person, I realized that nobody could free me from loneliness or make me feel like a good person who deserves to be loved. I understood that all my childish needs in closeness and acceptance that weren't met on time could not be satisfied by another person completely later in life. As an adult I was only able to satisfy my needs by finally starting to love myself. After many years of the search in the outside world, I finally found love within.

CHAPTER 3
WITHDRAWAL

Since the introduction to downhill skiing at the age of three, sport was a significant part of my life and gradually took over other parts. At some point, sport even became my whole life where everything was revolving around skiing. I didn't mind it at all because I enjoyed the feeling of uniqueness and achievements that I got from the sport. I didn't care about poor conditions for training. We used hand-made ski lifts and old gymnasiums. Our sports club's building didn't have a sewer and water connection, so there was no washroom. I was luckier than some of the other athletes because my parents tried their best to provide me with good equipment. For instance, I always had ski goggles when many other athletes didn't. I was happy with what I had for training because I couldn't compare my training environment with something different.

My dad and other coaches did a lot of work beyond their coaching responsibilities. I remember that I helped my dad and other coaches to repair the building of our sports club. I was around five years old and assisted them in sifting sand for cement. I enjoyed it and felt like a grown-up. The coaches put their time and efforts in building and repairing our sports club's building, in preparing slopes for a skiing season, installing and maintaining the hand-made ski lifts, and creating the best possible environment for training sessions.

Other athletes and I helped them to prepare slopes for the next season during some of the falls. We took saws and cut small trees that appeared on the slopes during the summer. We also needed to be vigilant about ski lifts during the training. The hand-made ski lift consisted of two big horizontal pulley wheels, one of which was located at the bottom of the slope and another one on the top. It also included a cable and around five in line, small towers with one vertical pulley in each direction. There were no T-bars attached to a cable. To go uphill, we had to attach our portable hooks to a moving cable that was scary to do when I was a child. That metal hook also had a rope and a narrow ten inches long piece of wood to put between legs and behind buttocks. At the top, after detaching the hook from a cable, we tied the rope around the waist and secured the wooden piece and the hook, so we can ski down and bring our hooks with us. There were three hand-made lifts. I was particularly scared of one of them. That ski lift didn't have enough towers at one of the sections to keep a cable at a proper height. Probably, there was not enough ground support to hold additional towers because that section was very steep. Athletes who were older and heavier than I didn't have trouble with riding that lift. I was too light that resulted in the lack of weight to keep a cable close to the ground. For a while the cable lifted me twenty inches up and I had to hold tight on the cable.

The danger of using that type of lifts was in the possibility of having a piece of clothes to wind around the cable. As a result, somebody could be stuck without a chance to escape a lift before the next pulley. We always watched other athletes, so we could approach the stop button on time and save somebody from injuries. There were also usual lifts with T-bars at our mountains. I don't know exactly why we didn't use them all the time. My suggestion is that our sports club couldn't always pay for lift tickets during the '90s, so we had to use our own lifts for training.

I remember as a little child putting my ski boots on and dreaming about the participation in the Olympic Games. Having eight training sessions per week, I worked hard to have success in sport. My dad was stricter to me than to other athletes. For example, during one of the competitions in a town close to Kirovsk, I had a very painful experience because he was upset that I didn't do the first run good enough. That day I participated in the slalom competitions, which always has two runs. After my not very successful first run, my dad prohibited me from using a ski lift. He wanted me to go all the way up to the start gates by feet caring my skis with me. It was an awful experience because I knew every athlete and coach at that competition was staring at me. I wished for the situation to end as fast as possible, but it was hard to go uphill in skiing boots and with skis on my shoulder. I was slowly climbing uphill hating myself for the bad first run and worrying about my next run. When I finally reached the start gate, my legs were shaking from tiredness. My second run wasn't very successful either.

I took many first places in my age category when I was doing downhill skiing. However, when I became a teenager, something changed. I wasn't able to progress in downhill skiing as fast as I did before. As a result, I couldn't take podiums anymore. It was a dramatic time for me because I had no idea what had happened and how to adjust to these changes. My dad was also upset with my results. I can't recall whose idea it was to try mogul skiing professionally. Downhill skiing and mogul skiing sections of our sports club were located in the same building. Since a very young age, I was familiar with that different type of skiing where you run down the heavily moguled course and also perform two jumps. I even tried it a little bit, but never trained for participation in competitions.

Deciding to give mogul skiing a try, I started to learn how to ski with different techniques and to jump. I was around fourteen years old at that time and it was hard to ski differently after many years of mastering techniques of downhill turns. Unfortunately, our coaches didn't know a lot of specific approaches in mogul skiing training. As a result, I had to learn the hard way: practice first runs on steep mogul course with high bumps and trying first jumps without knowing proper technique. However, after spending some challenging time on training in mogul skiing and overcoming my fears, I was able to take a podium in National Junior Competitions. Success came back to me and I was extremely happy. Since that time, I focused entirely on mogul skiing and then couldn't leave it for many years.

Sport meant so much to me: enjoyment, success, dad's acceptance, self-worth, opportunity to be noticed and valued. I couldn't imagine my life without sport and skiing. That is why for many years, sport has always been my drug. It took three times, three "I quit" to finally give it up. The first two times when I decidedly walked away from professional sport, the pangs and the general withdrawal was stronger than I was, and I relapsed.

The first attempt when I seriously decided to give up my sports career was in the last grade of high school. I craved for something new. Surprisingly, my father, who invested a lot in my sports career, took it well. There were no emotional outbursts or a plea to keep going. He shocked me by accepting my choice.

"Freedom!" I shouted inside, filling myself with an inner sense of delight. For the first time in my life, I could do what I felt like doing. It was new and exhilarating to have free time that I could spend in any way I chose and realize any dream.

"Dreams?" There was a moment when I realized that I didn't have any, or maybe they were buried away, but either way, I didn't know what I wanted. It was the pure irony that gifted with all this free time I didn't know what to spend it on. Freedom didn't seem as delightful as the promise of it did a moment ago. It actually felt alarming. All my life before that time I rarely thought about my desires. My mind was usually occupied by others, their needs and wants.

My Russian Way to Boldness

Looking back, I realize with a surprise that my life was very structured, and often I had no personal time to think about myself, my wishes, and my desires. From September to May, I had almost no days off. On weekdays I was busy with both school and training. The only day of the week when I didn't train was Monday. On each day of the weekend, we usually had two training sessions on the slopes. Today I wouldn't be able to maintain this kind of schedule, but back then, I had lots of energy: for school, training and even playing outside.

My training sessions didn't stop with the beginning of a school break. Summer break for schools in Russia lasts for three months: from June till September. Although I had more free time in the summer, a lot of it went into daily training sessions and into helping the grown-ups with the kitchen garden and other tasks. I was very responsible and couldn't drop my commitment to help out even if personally I really didn't want to assist my grandparents or parents. I was envious that my cousin had no trouble just leaving his tasks behind and going off to play with his friends. I wasn't like him. I felt needed and significant when I supported my family in any way I could. The desire to help out my grandma or grandpa was stronger than my need to play outside and hang out with friends.

I was always the last person I took care of. I helped my sister to do her homework, taking on the parenting role. I didn't ask my parents for pocket money or new clothes as I saw how hard they had to work for their wages. I tried to keep my needs to myself, so I wouldn't have to bother my parents. When I was a teenager, I needed new sneakers, and I decided to earn enough money on my own to buy them. When I was in the village during the summer, I went to the fields to pick a rare wild brambleberry. Then I sold it to the berries buyers that went from village to village. It took many hours to find and pick rare brambleberries, but I made enough money to buy the sneakers. When I got my first big cheque from my sports career, I bought a computer with a computer table, but not for me; they were for my dad and sister.

I also suppressed my emotions so as not to upset my family. At the time, their happiness was more important than my own. I was around them when they were sad or needed a shoulder to cry on, again and again, putting their needs above mine. I learned to be sensitive to the needs of others but forgot about mine. When I finally faced freedom that required me to live my own life, I was confronted by the fact that I did not really know myself.

Around the second semester of my senior year, it was time to decide on the next steps of achieving a bright future. I bought a thick dusty directory of universities and colleges around the country and flipping through the pages trying to decide on what career path was meant for me. Engineering – I never liked math, so it wasn't for me; doctor – diseases and blood make me queasy; police – I couldn't stand the rigid structure and rules. What about a sports coach? NO, there was no way I would be a coach like my parents. I kept flipping and eventually saw something interesting.

The faculty of International Relations seemed like a possible choice.

"Maybe I can be a diplomat," I thought. I always loved traveling, and a career in international politics seemed at least to offer a promise of excitement. I decided to apply to the faculty and started taking preliminary courses for the entrance exam.

A few months later friends of my parents came to visit from Moscow for the holidays. They stayed with us, and in the evenings, we drank black tea and talked just about everything. In one of these evenings, the topic was post-secondary education, and our friend Andrei was talking about his daughter applying to the education college in Moscow. I was always intrigued by the idea of teaching.

It brought me back to a memory when my sister and I played "school." We pretended to teach each other or be elementary school teachers together. It was always a fun and entertaining game. We didn't have a blackboard, so we had to improvise. We used paper and colourful sharpies, and a closet door which we covered with chalk marks. We pretended each of us had our own classroom full of students eager to learn. I remember standing at an improvised blackboard showing how to solve mathematical problems and talking about the wonders of the planets. During a break, my sister and I shared details of our previous lessons and very thoughtfully prepared for the next one.

All of a sudden, this delightful reverie was cut short by Andrei's question: "Elena, what are you planning to study? Maybe you can also enroll in college and study elementary school education."

"Me?.... Why not" I thought. "I like kids, and I like to teach. This sounds like a good idea."

After thinking about this option for a while, I asked for my parents' opinion. Mom and dad expressed a positive attitude towards this choice. This was it; it was decided that after graduation, I would go to Moscow to enroll in the education college which was located near one of the oldest and most famous Russian streets – Old Arbat. This historical street is renowned for innumerable gift shops, hordes of tourists and unique architecture that reminds people of a different time. I imagined my future where I would study in the center of Moscow, live in the city of cities, make new friends and dive into the cosmopolitan life. In July, I passed my entrance exams, got in and at the end of August it was time to leave my parents behind and go to Moscow.

I was standing at the train station waiting for the evening train that would take me away from the life I knew and into the unknown. My parents and my sister were standing next to me. At that moment I realized that my life was about to change forever, for real. It would never be the same again. On one hand, I was ecstatic about leaving my old life and diving into something entirely new and exciting; on another hand, I really wanted to stay home with my family. I couldn't believe, or more accurately, I couldn't process the fact that I was actually leaving.

Tears came to my eyes; I had no words to explain the pain and sadness I felt. Fear grasped me in a way I wasn't expecting, but I knew it was because of how close I had now become with my parents. We had finally achieved a closeness I had wanted all my life, and now I'm walking away from it. It was bitter and unfair. I spent all my childhood wanting to be this close especially with my mom and just when I got it, I had to give it up.

I was looking outside the train's window as trees and building slowly started to move, and my family rushed after the train to catch the last few glimpses of my face. We waved to each other and put forced smiles on our faces until we were no longer in view of each other. The train picked up speed rushing to take me into a new life, which I no longer wanted. I stood by the window for some time, looking at the darkness outside. There was so much tension inside of me. Grief and sadness seized me from head to toe. It felt as if the darkness of the outside seeped through the open crack of the window swallowing me. Eventually, my tears dried. I turned away from the window, entered my sleeping quarters, then closed the door to my past forever. Moscow was waiting.

I started classes and my new life in September. I was lucky to find a residence with Andrei's parents, an older couple that had an empty room in their apartment in an old building on the outskirts of Moscow. The first few months of attending the college, I felt elated by everything new: my first real experience living on my own, different classes and new classmates, a big city with infinite possibilities, and the free time to experience all of it. I was ecstatic by all these changes for a while. Eventually, the charm of everything new no longer excited me that much and finally, I was overcome with sadness.

Many things were different from my past experience. There were virtually no boys in our class, and the all-female company was weird to me even a little bit scary. I spent all my childhood with boys since downhill and mogul skiing was primarily male-oriented. I also didn't really know what to talk about with the girls in my group. They were different. Almost all the girls were from Moscow or surrounding suburbs and continued to live with their parents. They were so far removed from the world of sports, from trips to other cities and daily training, the world I was accustomed to. They simply didn't care to share my enthusiasm for the fast speed of skiing and pleasure from perfect turns. They couldn't relate to the thrill I felt on the slopes. None of them ever visited the north, and it was hard for them to imagine how life there could be different from urban life in Moscow that they were accustomed to. I made one close friend, but even spending time with her couldn't change my growing nostalgia.

My classes also weren't all that interesting. I began to dream about skiing, snow and competition. Every week, maybe every day, the want and desire to return to my old life grew stronger.

"What am I doing here?" I asked myself once while sitting in class. It felt as if I genuinely didn't know how I ended up in this life situation, so far from everything I knew and loved.

With the first signs of winter, I went into withdrawal. Dancing snowflakes in the air, fresh snow on the ground and crisps footprints on the snowy sidewalk - everything reminded me of skiing. During boring college classes, I would slip off into daydreaming about my exciting previous life of professional sports.

My former teammates had relocated to Moscow to continue their skiing career, and I met up with them. It only intensified my desire to go back. As the withdrawal grew stronger, I finally gave in. In December, I was clicking my ski boots into my skis. In order to continue training professionally, I had to join a new winter sports club in Moscow with a new coach. Luckily, this coach used to live in Kirovsk before coming to Moscow, and I knew him very well.

In December, I came back to skiing and already in January I was selected to go to my first Freestyle Europa Cup competition in mogul skiing. I was selected because I was one of the winners in the most recent Russian Junior Competitions. Taking time off training wasn't seen as a problem. What followed was placing in the top three in the Europa Cup, which led to the next level - the World Cup. This was a spectacular season for me, and coaches were equally impressed: I was drafted into the Russian National team. I continued to take classes at the education college, but due to constant traveling to training camps and competitions, I never managed to graduate.

My romance with skiing continued for four years until December 2008. During that period, I practiced my jumps and improved the technique of sharp turns through the bumpy slope specifically designed for mogul competitions. I was in top performance condition until the fateful day when just before the start of the World Cup, I did a routine jump and landed poorly crushing my right knee. The pain was excruciating. I was lying in the snow, unable to get up. I was terrified watching the First Aid staff drive up, and by the thought that this accident was something serious, something that would prevent me from competing. The pain in my knee subsided, but the pain-terror in my heart grew by the second. "What am I going to do now?" I was scared and lost lying on the stretchers that was taking me down the slope. The bright future I envisioned suddenly turned into a dark void. There was nothing there for me. Everything came crashing down in the few seconds of the jump.

I learned in the hospital that my Anterior Cruciate Ligament in my right knee was ruptured and I needed surgery. I was devastated by this news since I still naively believed it was something minor. I had to face the fact that instead of the World Cup for which I was preparing since the beginning of spring, I would spend the next six months recovering after the surgery and then another six months returning to the good enough physical conditions for competing.

I had the surgery about a month after I fell. My rehabilitation began right away, and I earnestly implemented all doctor's recommendations hoping to be back on the slopes as soon as I could be. Months followed, and in the middle of the spring, I returned to skiing. When I got on my skis, I felt a mix of fear and excitement as I was gently going down a flat hill for the first time since the surgery. Fortunately, I was able to prepare for the new season on time.

This was the Olympic season of 2009-2010, and I really wanted to go to the Vancouver Olympics. After the operation, it was harder to face the fear of jumps, especially since I never particularly enjoyed this part of a mogul course. I always preferred to go down the mogul bumps. Despite the fear and the icy course, I faced in Finland, where we went for the World Cup, I tried my absolute best during training. I was set to get into the Olympic team to represent Russia.

However, as the saying goes, 'it was not meant to be.' During one of the training sessions, I felt a sharp pain in my left knee when I did a turn. I was able to get off the mogul course and stop, but my knee refused to let my leg stretch out fully. My heartbeat quickened, and tension restrained my movements. I tried to distract myself from the thoughts of another knee trauma, but it was of no use. In the hospital after the MRI scan, a doctor said that a piece of meniscus tore off in my knee, and it was a good idea to surgically remove it since a loose piece could cause even more damage.

While I was heading back to the Finnish ski resort in the car, I experienced profound sadness and strong resentment. Other athletes at the resort were preparing for the upcoming World Cup competition, which I now knew I was not going to participate in. Instead, I was facing another surgery. I couldn't understand why life was so unfair to me, why I have to walk barefoot across the shards of my broken hopes again. They spread in all directions and stepping over them was more painful for me than thinking about my upcoming surgery. I knew from my first recovery experience that I was capable of moving through rehabilitation successfully. However, I had no idea what actions to take to keep me optimistic and not to give up. For me going through another disappointment and still maintaining hope was very challenging.

I was afraid to dream. Nothing was of interest to me. Potential chance of experiencing pain from failure and frustration one more time terrified and forced me to back away. The beautiful colours of the world faded and every new day didn't bode well for me. I spent some time after surgery in this gloomy state. Everything seemed meaningless. I wondered if it was time for me to move on and leave my dream about the Olympic Games behind. I thought about all other things that I would be able to do if I quit professional sports.

After the surgery, I went to my family in my native town near Finland. Recovery after meniscus repair was going to take a short time. It filled me with a positive attitude. "I don't care about failures! They will not stop me!" I became angry at some point while I was at home. Up to this moment, instead of anger, which was suppressed, I felt profound resentment. Finally, experiencing anger, I was able to break free from my negative attitude towards the future. I started to feel alive again. Approximately one month after that change in my attitude, I did the first run on the mogul course. Everything around me took on bright colours, and I awaited each new day with anticipation. The pain from my disappointment subsided, and I continued to dream, continued to believe in myself.

Though I couldn't make it to the Olympic Games 2010, I competed in Freestyle Europa Cup competitions instead. The final competition in that season was the Russian Freestyle Championship. I took first place and overshadowed my teammates who went to the Olympics. I was overjoyed! I was back in line and ready to train and compete.

However, the thought that was planted during my second recovery surprisingly came back. After two surgeries in a year, it was much more difficult to overcome my fears of jumps. Mogul skiing started to bring less fun and became more challenging. I thought if a few moments on a podium and the excitement of winning are worth all my efforts, maybe it was time to try something different. I dreamed of having a loving relationship. I also wanted to learn how to play guitar and sing.

I desired to visit other countries as a tourist instead of having a work trip as an athlete. In other words, I wanted a life beyond skiing.

After a few months, at the beginning of the summer, I got an unexpected job offer from the Russian Freestyle Federation. I was asked if I want to be a manager of the national ski-cross team (the discipline of freestyle). This turn of events astonished me. The offer was tempting because it gave me an opportunity to satisfy my other needs finally. However, life without being a professional skier frightened me too because I had no idea how to live it.

Ultimately, I took the risk and accepted the offer. My personal coach was very upset by this news. I'd recently won the Russian Championship and was in great condition. Not being sure if I made the right choice, I was also concerned. However, sudden changes in my life fascinated me, and I adhered to my plan. In the middle of the summer, I started my work in Moscow as a manager of the national team. Right away, I realized my ignorance of many elementary tasks such as writing an official email and using a printer. Also, the responsibility for the budget of thousands of dollars and for the preparation of important documents made me nervous.

Despite all difficulties with the new role, I persevered and with time, learned a lot about what it means to be behind the scene in Russian sport. Being financed by the government, Russian sports have advantages and disadvantages. As an athlete, I was able to take advantage of government support. I didn't pay for participation in the training camps and competitions, for buying sports equipment or for medical bills when I was injured. All these were covered by the government. As a manager, I also witnessed the disadvantages of the Russian sport - a rigid bureaucratic system. When I needed to adjust already approved plans for training camps, I had to spend a lot of time getting many signatures from the Ministry of Sports. The process was very slow, and I often couldn't keep up with the necessary changes in the training schedule of a team. After some time, I understood how difficult it was to change and improve anything in that system. If somebody is there, she or he just follows the rules. There is no opportunity to be a game-changer.

After a couple of months, I became used to my new responsibilities at work. After another few months, I started to feel bored. I craved for something bigger than routine paperwork. The rigid system I worked in didn't give me any chance for creativity.

One day, my colleagues and I were joking that even after many years at that job, we would still do the same tasks. As a result, we would turn into cantankerous old women. This thought never crossed my mind before. In a moment, it shook me up. Suddenly, I realized the truth behind this joke. If I didn't change this routine, I would be that person. Discomfort replaced my desire to continue as a manager. I knew almost immediately that the office job wasn't for me and I started to feel anxious.

In addition, life without skiing again wasn't as colourful as I imagined. Although I enjoyed the theatres and the museums, took painting lessons, played guitar and met with friends, I wasn't happy. As winter set in, I went into withdrawal.

At approximately the same time, I knew that our Freestyle Federation was going to hire Canadian coaches for the mogul team. This news made my withdrawal stronger because I was eager to experience the Canadian style of mogul training. Canadians are one of the best in mogul skiing in the world. After a couple of months, in February, I quit my job and resumed my training activities. I wanted to be back in the national team.

My spot in the team wasn't secured for me, but after some time, I proved myself to be there. Again, I was immersed fully in training camps and competitions. I trained in Canada, Russia, USA, Australia, Chile, Switzerland, Brazil and Mexico. For the first time in my sports career, there were so many training camps. Training for mogul skiing focuses on physical conditioning, on mastering turns and on improving jumps. Preparing my body for mogul skiing, I spent a lot of time in a gym and on the field. I not only strengthened my muscles but worked on improving my agility, power and endurance by doing numerous running and jumping exercises.

Improvement of my mogul jumps started with practicing them on a trampoline. Then I performed jumps at water ramp where I skied down the specially build ramp, jumped, and landed into the water with installed bubbles system. This system made landing on the water safer. After landing, I had to swim with my ski boots and skis on my feet to the edge of the pool where I could get out and put off my skis. To perform the next jump, I climbed the stairs to the top of the ramp. These training sessions required a lot of energy because I was constantly moving: jumping, swimming or climbing the stairs. We usually had two training sessions on a water ramp and one physical conditioning session every training day. Being tired after the full day of physical activities, I slept like a baby at night.

After improving my jumps on a water ramp, I practiced them on the snow: at first on an air bump separated from a mogul course and then on the air bumps on the course. I also worked on the techniques of my turns on groomed slopes and on moguls. Training season usually lasted from April till November. The final stage of every training season was about putting all elements together and practicing mogul runs from start to finish.

It was important to master turns, jumps and speed altogether because total scores for every run consists of three parts. Judges in the number of seven people pay attention to every element of an athlete's run. Fifty percent of the total score represents scores for turns, twenty-five percent for jumps, and another twenty-five percent for speed, which is the only objective parameter of a mogul run.

Because we had to train a lot and spent time in faraway areas that had snow during the summer, I sacrificed other aspects of my life even more than before. We were preparing for the Olympic Games in Sochi, and I dreamed of being on the Olympic team.

Training under Canadian coaches created a significant influence on me. I observed that they had a system of training we didn't have in Russia. I understood that they gradually led their athletes to the next level of excellence. For example, before jumping backflips on the trampoline, athletes learned the specific order of more simple skills to prepare for advanced movement. I had a different experience in my childhood. I was told just to jump backflip. It was so scary to do. Even though I was shaking inside, after a few moments, I jumped, but fear of jumps has stayed with me forever.

The way I learned mogul skiing in the past created enormous stress. Awareness of an easier way of training upset me. It was envious that Canadians athletes had something I didn't have. Nobody forced them to make their first mogul run on the steep and challenging course. They moved to their dreams gradually. Meanwhile, I constantly ended up in more difficult conditions where I had to push myself beyond the limits. Although I achieved great success, I still wondered what I could have achieved if I had that different type of mogul training since the beginning.

The Canadian coaches' training wasn't ideal, but it was much better than the training I had before. Nevertheless, I struggled with improving some elements of mogul skiing and with my confidence during competitions. The less time left until the Olympics, the more pressure I passed through. Three years before the Games were exciting but arduous at the same time. I not only had to get a spot in a Russian Olympic team but also needed to get my personal quote, which required me to rank in the top thirty female mogul athletes in a World Cup's overall ranking.

The participation in the Olympic Games 2014 was a reward for all my efforts. I spent many years trying to realize that dream and finally succeeded. Being on a national Olympic team, I was overwhelmed by joy! As other mogul teams, my team came to an Olympic Village one of the first because our competitions started even before the official opening of the Games. The village was half empty when we arrived. However, I was able to feel that unique sense of the Olympic Games. During our usual competition seasons, we almost didn't meet with athletes from other sports, but the Olympic Games gave us the opportunity to experience how sport brings people together.

Before competition days, we had a few training days to explore the mogul course and adjust to it because every course is different. Our coaches advised us not to use any social media during our time at the Olympic Games. I was surprised but followed their instructions. Later I realized that it was a smart decision because when I visited my social media accounts after the Olympics, I saw a huge number of messages. During the Olympic Games, I was extremely nervous. I worried about my runs and was afraid of getting injured right before the day of competitions. I trained my entire life for those few runs. The pressure I experienced was colossal. I definitely didn't need to put more pressure on myself by reading all messages that were supportive but could create more stress. Sometimes I even wished for the competition to finally be over, so I could relax a little bit.

I had a mixed experience from my participation in the Olympic Games. On one hand, it was exciting and unbelievable. On the other hand, I felt as stressed as I never felt before in my life. However, it was an experience of a lifetime that I will never forget. My dream finally came true!

I didn't know if the four more years of training until the next Olympics was something that I wanted. Such a significant commitment pushed me away. Again, I found myself at a crossroads. Past injuries manifested themselves. The older I became, the more effort was required for training. I also met a man I fell in love with. We wanted to be together and form a family. Besides that, I was also so tired from skiing and constant flighting here and there. All these factors restrained me from continuing my sports career.

At the same time, I realized my intense addiction to the sport. I felt like I was bound to it by a thick rope, which I couldn't cut. The sport wasn't my hobby or even my job. It was literally my life. From this solid connection, I got my significance, confidence, and my right to be accepted and loved.

I remember one day I was on the train at the Moscow subway. I looked at the people around me and noticed how usual and boring they were. I was in the national sports uniform. Just realization of the fact that I do mogul skiing, compete in high-level competitions and have a unique life made me feel significant. I was still lost in the thoughts about feeling special when suddenly anxiety was reflected on my face. I had another glance at the people that were sitting and standing around me and thought: "One day I will become like them." My teeth clenched, and my face muscles tensed. The idea of leaving sports forever boosted my anxiety. After all, the idea that my remarkable life as I perceived it was going to become common was incomprehensible to me. I was scared to be permanently deprived of feeling significant because I was nothing without sport.

For the first time, I fully realized that professional sport was in my life temporary. I was afraid of the future without sport and avoided thoughts about this perspective. Because I started to ski at three years old, I couldn't remember any time of my life without skiing and sport. I simply didn't see another way of living. It seemed to me that my life would be over if I stop skiing.

I truly believed that not only my significance would be gone together with sport but also my confidence. Everything was so evident in that sports world because I knew it since I was a child. I understood simple rules and necessary actions for success. Although this world didn't promise a win for everybody, I was accustomed to it.

In reality, without professional sports, I felt like a newborn baby among knowledgeable adults. Many of my peers by the age of twenty-seven had built relationships and family, worked at various places and gotten life experience. I knew very well only how to ski and felt unconfident in other areas.

Fortunately, the experience I gained working as a manager supported me. Even though the management position was related to sports, it was still an entirely different life. "That time I couldn't bear the withdrawal. Maybe I will be able to go through it now." I wondered. In addition, I understood that either now or later time to leave profession sport forever would come. My body has limited resources. I knew one rule from other athletes' experience – the longer you are involved in the sports, the more difficult adapting to a new life becomes.

For me, acceptance and love from my family also were depended on my sports achievements since childhood. I really believed in conditional love. Sports success was one of the conditions. By all means, I tried to merit acceptance from my parents. I wanted to be the best at the competitions. Actually, I dreamed of being the best for my dad. I didn't handle losing very well because it meant the end of receiving love from him.

The sport was my drug, and I was addicted to it. I was torn between all the benefits of sports and the things that were missing in my life. After a proposal from my boyfriend one month after the Olympic Games in 2014, I decided to quit the sports for the third time. It was February again. I don't know why but all three times I quit sports career at that time of the year. It seemed like an important month for me. I am wondering if it is just a coincidence that my dad also has his birthday in February.

When the competition season of 2014 was over, I left the sport. What came next were the many colourful events: a relocation to Canada, my wedding, honeymoon, and married life. Sadness from being far away from my family and friends was compensated by the new stunning experiences I had.

However, as probably it could be predicted, I started to have withdrawal symptoms once again. I had dreams about training and competition a few times every week. I woke up thinking: "Maybe it is not too late to go back?" The sport beckoned me to be an athlete.

This time supported by my husband and my counsellor, I had the strength to resist my addiction to the sport. My husband Ivan gave me his love and care. He also evoked my desire to be with him instead of being far away, participating in competitions. My counsellor assisted me in understanding myself. I realized there were many alternative ways to satisfy my needs that in the past, were only fulfilled by being an athlete. Nevertheless, for two years after retirement, I continued to have dreams about skiing and still had a desire to compete again.

Gradually withdrawal became less and less intense until it transformed into light nostalgia. Working with my counsellor, I discovered that I am significant just because I exist. In the whole world, there is no person identical to me. It turned out that the right to feel unique is a birthright. I need do nothing to be special. This simple thought gave me a great relief.

This idea wasn't natural for me at first. I recognized the fact that during my childhood, I rarely heard from my parents "I am glad to see you" or "I missed you so much." Without this acknowledgment, I, as any other child, couldn't feel recognized and special. Instead, I had to put a lot of effort in order to be seen, gradually understanding that I needed to continue proving myself in exchange for being loved. In my case, it was about winning at sports.

Excelling at school, being at constant help to parents, having a beautiful appearance, playing piano at a superior level are other ways for a child to prove to parents that she/he is good. Unfortunately, all those efforts usually do not bring an inner sense of oneself as of a lovable person. I still sometimes struggle with maintaining this feeling of self-worth in challenging situations. The first step to a new attitude towards myself was to realize that I used my sports achievements to get recognition from my parents. This understanding helped me to initiate changes in my behavioral patterns.

During meetings with the counsellor, I also observed the relationship with my parents from a different perspective, from the more rational point of view. I recognized their unconditional love, which they simply couldn't demonstrate in my childhood. I understood they loved me unconditionally even though it didn't look like it when I was a child. The only one who still resisted to accept me unconditionally was me. I was and sometimes still harsh on myself more than anybody else. Instead of focusing on other people and their acceptance, I gradually started to shift focus to my attitude towards myself.

After leaving sport, I was surprised to see that the world was larger and more diverse than I thought. Many opportunities opened its doors for me. Before, I was like a horse with the blinders, seeing only one way. When blinders were removed, I was able to observe a variety of ways to live. My addiction to the sport was gone.

CHAPTER 4
WHO AM I?

After retirement from professional sports, I felt totally lost. Everything that was meaningful to me became unimportant. Leaving my career, moving to a new country, starting a married life – all these forced me to face the question "Who am I now?" There was a silence in my head instead of the answer.

During my previous years, I became used to thinking about myself as an athlete, freestyle skier and a member of a national team. Because of my constant focus on others and sport, I also had no idea whom really I wanted to become, what I liked and what I desired to do next. Losing the ground beyond my feet, I struggled to determine my new identity. My inner map was just partially explored by me. However, this very well-known part of my identity – an athlete – was left in the past. I was grieving for that part, but at the same time, I was trying to explore other parts of me. The idea that I didn't know myself stuck me. As a result, exploring and discovering my true Self became one of my missions.

The problem was that I didn't only quit my career but went through many transitions at the same time. The change in my profession led to a colossal transformation of my overall lifestyle. For example, incorporating physical activity into my daily life never was my problem before because it was my job. After leaving sports, for the first time, I met with the challenges of a sedentary lifestyle. Now I have to make conscious efforts to stay physically active.

However, to determine my new social part of my identity was the easiest for me. Being an athlete was replaced by being a wife, a personal trainer, and a business owner. Belonging to many new large and small social groups helped me a lot in understanding who I was. Being a member of different organizations and networking events, I was able to fill some of the gaps in my identity.

During many years in sports, I had constantly been travelling. I didn't have a permanent home in Russia because I didn't spend a lot of time there between my training camps and competitions. I left my parents' home after my graduation from high school and since that time, I had only temporary places to stay. I am talking here not only about a house or a condo, but also more generally about the place – a city and community - I could call home. I didn't settle down in any specific place.

Of course, this situation changed when I moved to Canada. After a few years here in a particular place, in addition to being Russian, I started to identify myself as a Canadian, an islander and a member of many communities. For the first time, I felt sad leaving this country when my husband and I went to Russia for a vacation after being in Canada for three years. That summer I realized that I was leaving my home – my city, my community, my friends and my Canada.

I still love Russia. However, this is the type of love somebody experiences towards their hometown. She comes to that place for a short visit from time to time. Everything is so familiar, but at the same time so alien. During those visits, she understands that she does not belong there anymore. She can't stay there for a long time and is happy to return to her new permanent home.

However, there were also some traps in my social

identification. I easily felt into rigid social beliefs. For instance, I tried to be a good wife in the way that I imagined it to be. For me, it meant to do all home chores by myself and to please my husband. It took some time to understand that this belief didn't do me any good. Otherwise, being "good wife" created a lot of tension and stress.

We were meeting with our friends when one of them talked about his struggles with independent living after he moved out from his parents. Other guys agreed with him that he just needed to get a wife and won't have to worry about cleaning, cooking and other house chores anymore. At that moment, I said nothing. After we left, I realized my irritation. I was saying to my husband how unfair it is to expect from a wife to do everything at home and to work at the same time. For a few days, I had been thinking about that situation and my friends' comments. Then I finally understood that my irritation actually signaled me about my own situation at home where I did most of the house tasks.

I did it not because my husband didn't want to help me, but because I believed that to be a good wife, I had to do everything myself. I often felt guilty if I didn't have time or energy to accomplish something at home and at the same time, experienced frustration of having too much on my shoulders. It was time to break free from my "good wife" belief and talk to my husband. We decided to split our house chores. It became easier for me to ask him for help. Although it was difficult to see how he did everything in his way, I stayed silent. I remembered that in my childhood, I always wanted to help my grandma with cleaning or cooking. However, she couldn't stand that I cleaned the floor or cut vegetables the "wrong" way. As a result, she asked me to stop and then continued herself, leaving me feeling sad and worthless. I didn't want my husband to experience the same emotions that I did. So, I learned to tolerate my feelings, let my control go or simply retreat to another room. Today, I still struggle sometimes with letting him do house chores or anything without feeling guilty that I didn't do that task myself. However, my "good wife" belief is less rigid now that helps me to overcome any struggles.

Another part of my identity – personal dimension – was more difficult to discover than the social one. I knew just a little about what I wanted and liked. The large piece to it was missing. I had to start an exploration of this part with small steps. I learned to be more aware of my daily life experiences and because of it, I began to notice how different things, activities and situations affected me.

For example, surprisingly, I realized that I don't like the taste of black tea. One day I was recommended by my naturopathic doctor to cut my dairy intake. I love dairy products and also was used to drinking black tea with milk. I couldn't give up on cheese and yogurts, but to remove milk from my tea was realistic. To do so mindfully, I asked myself why I drink tea with milk in the first place. It was interesting to discover that I simply do not like the taste of black tea. The second question was why I drink it daily if I have to use milk to mask its taste? After some thinking, I realized that, firstly, in my family in Russia, drinking black tea was a part of daily life. I never called this tradition into the question. Secondly, my husband is a black tea drinker. When we started to live together, drinking black tea became a shared activity with my husband. The realization of small things described above was one of the ways for being more mindful and discovering myself. It was and still is the process of adjusting my habits and thinking patterns to new discoveries I make about myself. For example after the discovery about black tea, I started drinking herbal teas.

By trying new things and exploring various opportunities, I was able to find what I like and dislike. In the past, I thought about myself as a person who doesn't like to be at public events and meet new people. Well, while living in Victoria, I discovered that I like to be active in a community and to visit networking events. I also realized that I love psychology and learning in general. However, regularly I also need to put all my mind activities and social life aside and simply go to the nature.

Finally, by writing my blog posts, I learned that I love sharing my ideas and experiences with people via writing and public speaking.

To understand my wishes was a hard activity for me. For instance, when my husband and I was walking downtown on one hot summer day, I bought an ice-cream. After eating it, I realized that in reality, I didn't want an ice-cream. I was just very thirsty but couldn't recognize that need at the beginning. With time, because I regularly asked myself what I wanted even in a small action such as what to eat for breakfast, what to do over the weekend, what to wear today, I developed a better understanding of my wishes and desires, including the big ones. As a result, I became more confident and at peace.

In my physical dimension of identity, I faced many challenges too. When I retired from sports, my body decided to get back at me for all the years I used it as a tool for my successes in sports. I had to accept my new identity of the person with low back pain and migraines. This acceptance gave me an opportunity to explore what physical activities my body likes after many years of intense training. I tried yoga, Tai chi, different types of dancing, rocket sports and so on. Giving myself a chance to move differently and with awareness during those activities, I connected with my body much more than before and learned a lot about myself. However, the most challenging was to identify myself as a bald person after my alopecia progressed and I lost most of my hair. Am I still a woman if I do not have long hair? What stance to take towards my baldness? Do I identify myself with my disease or this is just a part of me? Do I like my new look? All these questions pumped up in my head requiring answers. Fortunately, I was able to deal with that situation eventually and use my baldness in a positive way. For instance, when I schedule a meeting with somebody who doesn't know how I look, I can name my appearance's feature without any hard feelings by saying, "I am bald." In this case, a person can easily recognize me.

I also was exploring my relationships with nature, volunteering work and being in the present moment – as psychologist says with my spiritual part of identity. The connection between nature and my panic "attack" became obvious. I put the word attack in quotes because I have never been diagnosed with having panic attacks. However, the symptoms I experience during the time of my panic are very similar to the description of panic attacks. I noticed that when I regularly spent time outdoor without rushing somewhere, my panic diminishes.

Although mindfulness and time with myself bring me relaxation and pleasure, I find it difficult to initiate this type of activity. My former identity was all about engaging or doing one thing or the other. I played social roles, focused on accomplishments and hobbies often without being present in the moment. I am working towards shifting more towards being present-minded because I believe that being here and now and having meaning is the basis for a fulfilled life and happiness. I am not surprised that in our fast pace world mindfulness came into play for many people.

When I was looking for the answers to the question of who I was, I came across one of the social media posts about genealogy. Even before this, I had an interest in learning more about my roots. However, I never pursued it hard enough to find many details about my ancestry. That day I decided to enroll in a five-week online course, which was a mix of genealogy and psychology. The big part of the course was to feel a connection with my ancestry, understand family myths and accept unpleasant parts of my ancestry's history. The combination of finding new information about my relatives and processing it mindfully was what I needed.

During my childhood, I formed some beliefs about my extended family. For instance, I was sure that it is not appropriate to ask my paternal grandfather about his parents. I knew that my grand-dad and one of his sisters had different fathers. Being curious to learn more, I also felt it's a taboo to ask these questions. When I finally decided to have a discussion with my relatives about that topic, to my biggest surprise, they were open to talking about it. It turned out that my great-grandparents both lost their partners from the first marriage. There weren't any dark secrets as I imagined. Although I felt slightly upset by the absence of any secret, I experienced relief from learning more about my roots.

For some time, I couldn't understand why my relatives never talked about their past in detail. While I was searching for more information, I realized why it was a case. The situation in USSR affected the relationship between family members in a specific way. People often preferred to keep facts about their past or family private. They didn't share them even with their partners. My paternal grandparents had been together for more than fifty years. When my grandmother was still alive, I called them to clarify some data I found online. I wasn't sure if I discovered the records about my great-grandfather or not at one of the websites about The Second World War soldiers.

"Granny, does your father-in-law, my great-grandad, serve in the army during the war?" I asked with curiosity after exchanging usual greetings.

"Hm, no. He didn't participate in the war. He was just weak," my granny answered, making me confused. The name on the record was an exact match. The region that was noted as a place of birth was the same as the place my great-grandfather lived in.

"It is so strange! Ok, I will call back when grandpa is home" I was determined to resolve my doubts.

After some time, I called my grandparents again. My grandpa was at home. I explained the situation and the records I found. When I heard my grandpa's answer, I was shocked.

"Yes, he served for the duration of the war. He even had medals. You know, he was also shot a few times, but survived." The answer that I didn't expect to hear after talking to my granny.

I couldn't get it. Why my grandmother didn't know that

basic information? Did they never talk about it for fifty years of being together!? I couldn't imagine myself and my husband without discussing our parents. It should be a reason behind their silence.

I learned that the situation in USSR was very unsafe. Anybody could be easily arrested without any reasons especially in the thirties of the twentieth century. Police could come at any moment and take you away. You would be put into prison but most likely into the labour camp with inhuman conditions in the far part of the USSR. In the worst-case scenario, you would be killed together with hundreds of other people. At the same time, your family would be labeled as a family of a traitor, kicked out of the home and sent to an exile in a different region.

I discovered that there was an awful accident in the village where my maternal grandfather grew up in. He had an auntie who lived with her family in the same village. The auntie had two daughters under ten years old and was expecting a third child. Her husband was a fisherman, just like other men in that village. Commercial fishing was one of the main sources of employment. This family was a usual family living in their own small house and working hard to survive.

One night in March 1938, they were waked up by the knock at their door. The event that many soviet people consciously or unconsciously was afraid of happened. The father of the family was arrested right away. His wife and daughters never saw him again. He was put into the prison and executed a few months later, on May 8th, 1938. Nobody knew where he was buried and if he was buried at all. His family was exiled and for many years treated as the family of a traitor. The youngest daughter died shortly because of the hard-living conditions the family was put into. Fortunately, the newborn child was able to survive.

The same night in March 1938, another twenty-nine men in that village were arrested for the same accusation. They were accused of being spies and all killed in May 1938. Many families suddenly lost their fathers, husbands, sons and brothers that night. Were those men spies? Of course, not. In 1959 USSR government admitted that accusation was false and exculpated all thirty men.

I heard a rumor that a person who was a head of the municipality of a village at that time got an order from a superior organization to find thirty suspicious and unreliable residents. He and a few other people in management positions handwrote a list of thirty randomly selected male residents of the village. Shortly those men were arrested and killed. Some people who grew up in that village and whom I met strongly believe that list was the only reason for arrests. One lady also said that life punished all of those who made the list.

Another true story that was shared to me by my maternal grandmother about her father, my great-grandfather, who was an engineer. He and his family lived in a region close to Saint-Petersburg. At some point, he was offered a job at one of the factories in Siberia. His wife agreed to give living in another city a try, and shortly they moved to Siberia. When summer arrived, his wife and two daughters went on a vacation, visiting relatives in their home region.

My great-grandfather unexpectedly came there later, saying that he was going to stay for a few weeks. However, when two weeks passed by, he didn't leave. Days went by, but he still stayed there. He was reluctant to talk about that situation. Finally, his wife was able to get an answer to her concerns about his strange behaviour. It turned out that he almost got arrested in Siberia. One day he was coming to his work a little bit later than usual when he met one of his co-workers near the factory. The co-worker was extremely nervous. He said that my great-grandfather must leave urgently without going to his work place; arrests were being made, and it was a suicide to go there.

My great-grandfather hesitated for a moment as he couldn't believe that it was happening for real. He decided to run away and left that city because he knew that nobody was granted normal human rights at that time in USSR. He never went back to that city and, fortunately, nobody looked for him in his hometown.

I can't imagine how it was to live in such a condition with total absence of safety and stability. It makes sense that in that environment, people didn't share information even with their immediate family members. It was dangerous to talk about yourself, your family and your background. If you kept information only to yourself, you had higher chances to survive during repressions. Probably, being very private became a habit for my relatives. That is why my grandmother didn't know about her father-in-law, and many stories were never told to grandkids.

My great-grandparents were born at the beginning of the twentieth century. They lived through the First World War, Russian Revolution, repressions, hunger, and The Second World War. All four of my great-grandfathers participated in the Second World War and survived. As I understand, I am very lucky none of them died because many men didn't return home. Their children, my grandparents, were hit by the war when they were little. They saw a lot of suffering and pain — what a harsh and awful time to live in. I feel like crying anytime I imagine how it would have affected me if I had lived in that period.

Knowing more about psychological traumas, the importance of early attachment between a parent and a child, and the role of emotions, I came to an understanding of what they might have faced. Of course, they didn't have a chance to visit a counsellor. Nobody talked to them about post-traumatic stress disorder. My great-grandparents and grandparents didn't have everything I have in my life to support me. How strong and resilient they were in dealing with everything on their own! I feel unbearable sorrow thinking about what they sacrificed just to keep going with their lives and about the heaviness they felt in their souls.

During the Second World War, my paternal grandfather

Sergey was between six and ten years old. He lived with his family in a small village in the central part of Russia. When German soldiers entered that village, they occupied the house of Sergey's family. For some period of time, my grandfather lived in the same house with German soldiers. He doesn't like to talk about that experience. However, there was one story he told a few times.

At that period, his youngest brother was a newborn. Of course, he couldn't control his behaviour as the oldest kids did, so he cried when he was hungry. Unfortunately, it happened often because his mother didn't have enough food to eat and as a result, there wasn't enough milk to feed him. One day, one of the soldiers who was younger than the others couldn't tolerate the cry anymore. He stood up from his military radio station, quickly grabbed his raffle with a bayonet in one hand and Sergey's little brother in another hand.

Ready to kill, he pointed his bayonet towards a little boy. Suddenly, another older German soldier stopped him. After a short conversation in German, the raffle was put aside, and Sergey's brother continued to live. It is difficult to process what a seven years old boy experienced, watching how his younger brother almost got killed.

Knowing this story and imagining how the war affected my grandfather, I wasn't surprised to discover that he dropped out of college in later years because of the German language course. How many painful memories could that course evoke in him? Of course, I don't know exactly if his childhood experience was the only reason he refused to take that required course or not. However, I assume that not only him, but all my grandparents suffered to some degree from memories and feelings from their childhood they carried all their life.

When I explored the life of my grandparents, I began to understand their behaviour and why they acted in a certain way. I become closer and more connected to them. I also gained more compassion and understanding towards my parents. They definitely were affected by the traumas of their parents, who went through the war.

There were questions I never asked. It simply didn't cross my mind, for example, to ask my father about his relationship with his grandparents. We never discussed his childhood from this perspective. I opened a totally new side of my father after I finally asked him to tell me something about his maternal grandma and grandpa. It turned out they were emotionally attached to him. He went to visit them regularly when he was a child. My great granddad taught him how to fish and create things by hands. My great-grandmother was always happy to see him and cooked pancakes for him. Although they didn't express their love a lot, they truly cared for him. Unfortunately, my father didn't have a close relationship with his paternal grandparents. They lived far away and even when my father went there a few times, they didn't show a lot of affection.

Some other stories about my ancestors are really fascinating. For example, one of my great-great-grandmothers Ulyana gave birth to nine sons. My great-grandfather, who later became an engineer and escaped arrest was her youngest son. Having so many kids, Ulyana still continued to work at a textile factory. Her first workday was when she was eight years old and the last one more than fifty years later. All her life, she worked hard at the factory and at home. Unfortunately, the wars didn't come around her family. Five of her sons died in the battles.

Another great-great-grandmother Olga from my mother's side had a lot of twists in her life story. She lost her parents at a very young age and was partially adopted by the rich owner of a factory. I say "partially adopted" because she was provided with the place to live and even could eat at the same table with him and his family; however, she still had to do all the work that servants did. She was a part of the family but wasn't their daughter.

When Olga was around eight years, they sent her to Saint-Petersburg, where she helped at a pharmacy. She had been living there till sixteen years old when suddenly the marriage was arranged for her. She saw her husband Pavel for the first time in the church on the day of the wedding. He was fifteen years older than she was.

After the wedding, they left Saint-Petersburg and moved to one of the villages in the nearby region. Four children were born in the next ten years. Even though Olga and her husband had an arranged marriage, he loved her very much. One day he was coming home from work when one of his neighbours told him heartbreaking news that his entire house burned to ashes. Without remembering himself, Pavel ran to his house, but nothing was there. Only burned wooden pieces were left. He barely could stand on his feet. His imagination showed to him that his wife and children were burned in the fire.

He didn't know at that time that his family was able to escape the house and survived. The shock was so severe that even the news that everybody was alive couldn't calm his mind. He became sick and died shortly.

Olga, with four kids was left without a husband and a place to live. She didn't have any job and any relatives to help her. Understanding that she couldn't support herself and the kids, she sent her three daughters to the monastery. They were old enough to live there for a while. The youngest child, a son, stayed with her. To earn money, Olga moved to her hometown and started to do all types of housework for other people. She didn't make a lot of money, but it was enough to have some food and a place to stay.

After a few years of struggles, Olga met a man with whom she fell in love. He was a baker in his own bakery. They started to live together, and Olga, finally, was able to take her daughters out of a monastery. Her new husband was very kind to her kids. Life became easier for all of them.

Learning this and other information expanded my understanding of my relatives and their relationship. How was it to raise nine sons without washing machine, fridge and so on? How was it to be left alone with four kids without any social support? How did they manage to work so hard, went through extremely hard times and still had a sense of humor?

I definitely began to appreciate my current life more after I got to know my relatives' stories.

Some facts about my family were discovered by me accidentally, some facts I obtained after hours of searching. The work on my family tree gave me not only more knowledge about my roots but also a lot of support. Although I became more aware of my ancestry's weaknesses, for example, co-dependence between family members, difficulties in expressing their feelings, broken relationships, I also learned more about their strengths. They all had something that supported them such as humor, kindness, music, interests, curiosity and so on. Definitely, all of them were resilient. I learned from church records that at that time, almost half of the kids died at an early age. To grow up was already a success. So, my great-grandparents and so on were very resilient and strong people. They are part of me, and I am part of them. Being their descendant, I can access this resilience, strength and other characteristics that support me in life.

In discovering my roots, I discovered myself. I was able to make my identity stronger. During the five-week genealogy course I took, we did a few visualizations. One of them was about imagining myself in front of all my relatives from the other generations. It was a very powerful exercise! I was able to feel the connection with all of them. The understanding that so many people stand behind my back and support me became very empowering.

CHAPTER 5
BODY AS A TOOL

During the conversation with some of my friends, I discovered they believe that athletes are perfectly in tune with their bodies. I had been pondering over their words and finally realized why my friends have this opinion. The exceptional connection with the body seems evident for an elite athlete to have. But this is only partly applicable.

I can't speak for everyone, but my experience convinced me that good control over the body doesn't guarantee hearing its messages well. On the one hand, I sensed my muscles and coordinated them with no trouble. On the other hand, during my sports life, I learned not to pay attention to pain, fatigue and feeling unwell. My body was my job tool. There was a training schedule I had to follow. There were competitions, to which I wanted to be prepared. If something went wrong in the body, doctors tried to fix those minor issues as fast as possible. Breaks in the training process could be critical for success at competitions.

Of course, major problems with my health happened too. Longer recovery time and rest were necessary at those moments. However, while my body was recovering, I was depressed and angry at my body for its break down.

Occasionally, I gave some relaxation time to my body even if there were no problems with my health, but those periods were very insignificant and didn't nourish my body to the necessary level.

When I was a little child, I had a solid connection with my body and heard its messages. Every child has this skill. As I moved toward adolescence, I gradually shifted to treating my body as an object, which helped me in achieving my goals. While participating in the sport, I couldn't miss the training days because of my period and not feeling my best. I didn't allow myself to respond to the distress and didn't stop until the pain was extreme.

Genuine contact with my body and body acceptance was lost somewhere in my childhood. In addition to sport, there were other aspects of my life that affected my body image and my connection with the body.

When I was eight years old, I had a surgery. After that time, I started to hate doctors. Of course, when I grew up, I changed my perspective on doctors. However, the traumatic experience was imprinted in my memory forever. This event happened during the fall. I was put into the hospital, as I was told that it was necessary for treating my breathing. Sometimes, it was tricky for me to breathe through my nose, but it didn't bother me. At first, I spent some time in a hospital, having treatments. I shared a room with, maybe, four other girls. One of them was very nice. We played together even though she was older than me. I also remember having a study book for English which I enjoyed, because all the characters there were from Disney Cartoons.

I don't recall how long I spent in the hospital, but my family came to visit me a few times. During one of those visits, my little sister was crying at the end because she wanted me to go home with her. With all my heart, I wished to go with her, but I had to stay at the hospital.

The surgery was a huge surprise to me. Maybe, my mom told me about the upcoming surgery, but I couldn't grasp the meaning of that word entirely. I didn't expect any pain or suffering. One day, a nurse came to my room and said that a doctor wanted to do some tests. Without any negative thoughts, I went with her to a doctor. However, we passed the usual treatment room and continued to walk in the long hall. At first, I wasn't suspicious. But it changed when we finally entered a room. There wasn't a lot of furniture. I saw a very strange chair and metal tools on a small table. Those tools made my heart rate go up. I felt that my body was grabbed by fear.

The doctor asked me to sit on that weird chair. When I did as he wanted, he took some tool, but not a metal one, and asked me to open my mouth. Then he applied something inside my throat. He also looked inside my throat for a while, making me very nervous. Suddenly, the nurse tied up my legs and arms to the chair. I had no idea how to react! I couldn't move and was in a panic. Nobody was there to help me.

The doctor took a metal tool that consisted of a long handle and a ring at the end. After the nurse grabbed my head from behind and pulled it back, the doctor inserted that scary metal tool into my mouth. A few seconds later, I felt excruciating pain in my throat. Blood gushed out from my nose and mouth. I was crying and trembling. Through my tears, I noticed small bloody parts of my body – adenoids – on the metal tray. They were just pulled out of my throat. The nurse tried to wipe the blood from my face, but I was shaking my head from side to side.

"Stop your cry!" the doctor said angrily. "It isn't a big deal." His behavior didn't reflect any empathy.

I was smashed by his words. "Why is he talking like this? Why did they do it to me? What is happening?" I thought and couldn't stop crying. The nurse, finally, was able to wipe the blood from my face. Then she released the ropes on my legs and arms. In addition, she said that I shouldn't eat for a while, but she soon would give me an ice cream.

The way back to my hospital room disappeared from my memory. When I entered the room, I lay down on my bed and entirely covered up with a blanket. My family wasn't there. I wished somebody could soothe me, but I was alone. That day something changed in me. I felt that I was betrayed by the nurse, who was initially nice to me, and my family. I lost trust. My body didn't belong to me anymore. The pillow on my bed became wet from my tears. The physical pain decreased after a while, but my emotional pain stayed with me much longer. It was one of the pivotal moments in forming my attitude toward my body. It taught me that a situation when I and my body were treated without respect was normal.

My relatives, unfortunately, also played a significant role in my negative attitude toward my body. For instance, in my childhood, there was a time when my father unpleasantly commented about my body. For some period, he criticized the way I walked. He didn't like that my feet were pointed a little bit out when I made steps. My father also didn't like the way I breathe in certain moments or situations. When he said with disgust: "Again you breathe like this!" I couldn't grasp the reason for his disgust and irritation. I simply didn't know what to answer. My long hair also occasionally irritated him. I assume that he was worried for my safety during the training sessions. The skiing lifts were handmade and weren't safe. Maybe he was afraid that my hair could wind up on the cable. In that case, I would not be able to get off on time and escape dangerous top lift pulley. However, when he was angry and told me that he was going to cut my hair eventually, I felt ashamed.

What could I do with my body and physiology? Yes, I could cut my hair, but I wasn't able to change the way I walked or breathe. My father's requests, probably coming from the good motives, were unrealistic. I couldn't change my body and felt that something was broken in me.

Another unpleasant experience happened when I visited my grandmother. She often forced me to eat more than I wanted. Probably, feeding others, especially grandkids, was a manifestation of her huge love. However, every time she insisted on more food on my plate, I had to suppress the natural regulatory mechanism of my body. In childhood, I could barely resist her attempts to feed me. I had to turn off the feeling of fullness in my stomach in order to please her.

In addition, a few times, I was hit by my relatives. It happened very unexpectedly. I know that some people were constantly subject to physical abuse in their families. In my case, it happened only twice. However, I vividly remember those moments.

I understand that in moments of distress, adults can do harmful things to their children. If they are not regular abusers, later they regret their uncontrollable emotional actions. The worse thing is not that they did things such as slapping their child, but that they didn't accept their wrong actions. Saying sorry is crucial in this type of situation. By saying, "Sorry, I was wrong. I shouldn't have done this to you," they legitimate child's feelings and help he/she to get through painful experience. Again, it only works when an adult is not a regular abuser. In the situation, when an adult constantly says sorry but continues to act harmfully, his/her words lose any healing power and become a mock. Unfortunately, my relatives never said sorry for their actions. That is why those two times of physical abuse in the form of hits contributed to my negative attitude towards my body and myself.

Being a child, I didn't think about the consequences of those traumatic experiences. Until many years later, I was able to understand that those events were one of the reasons I allowed other people to treat my body and myself poorly.

Of course, I treated myself the same way too. I wasn't kind and compassionate to myself. For the first time, my body protested against cruel mistreatment in puberty. The body made its voice heard by a headache. During some period, I felt intense pain in my forehead from time to time and wasn't able to train. Instead, I had to lie on a handcrafted couch in the sports school's room.

Eventually, regular headaches were gone as sudden as they

began. It gave me joy, but my body didn't quit its attempts in reaching out to me. Once I went to school with two ponytails instead of one as I usually did. During the break between classes, my classmate pointed out that something was wrong with my hairstyle at the nape area. I was astonished and couldn't understand what she was talking about. I also wasn't able to check it by myself. After coming back home, the first thing I asked my mom was to have a look at my nape. Mom's words after her observation sounded scary: 'There is a bald patch there".

I struggled with accepting this fact. My mom couldn't explain why I started to lose my hair at thirteen years of age when I was absolutely healthy. We went to the GP doctor, who referred me to different specialists and tests. I visited a neurologist, gynecologist, and endocrinologist. A lot of blood was taken for tests. I went through a very unpleasant test – gastroscopy. I also had ultrasound procedures. My fear grew bigger and bigger until it reached its peak during one of the meetings with the endocrinologist.

It was a final visit, and I was ready to know the diagnose. My mom and I entered the doctor's office and sat on uncomfortable chairs. The doctor began to explain to my mom test results, which I couldn't fully understand. Suddenly, the doctor's comment, in a monotone voice, frightened me a lot. My world started to collapse when I heard: "Your child has to stop participating in the sport."

"For how long?" my mom asked.

"Forever" the doctor answered with an icy voice.

I have a knot in my stomach. I am shocked by the possibility of leaving the sport, which meant everything to me. I imagine a gloomy existence in the future. I freeze in front of the doctor, as a wounded animal, unable to escape stiffens in front of a hunter. Everything shudders inside. The hunter points a gun to the target. "Bang" he shots again to kill the prey. "Bang" and the doctor says: "Also all her life she will have to take pills."

I clung to the chair; my lips pursed tightly. I can't speak. The second shot killed something inside me. I am not bleeding, but I am losing my hope, my dreams, the meaning of my life. My future is killed outright.

I craved to scream with anger and despair, but I just continued to look from the doctor to my mother, experiencing horror. I imagined my future life limited by permanent dependence on pills. I also panicked thinking about life without sport. Such a future seemed dreary and doomed. While I was engrossed in my thoughts, my mom ended the conversation with the doctor, and we left the office. Everything appeared unreal.

That day I did not know the diagnosis. The doctor couldn't say what exactly was happening with me. However, she insisted on the pills for my thyroid. During the medical testing, a possible reason for hair loss was detected only in the thyroid. Some hormone levels were near the lower range.

I had no idea how to live after that awful visit to the doctor. There was no hope for me in the future. My mind was foggy, and I couldn't think. I was terribly depressed but tried to look normal.

Fortunately, I didn't have to mourn my dead future for long because my parents were able to reanimate it. My mom decided not to stuff me with the hormones. After a while, I quit taking pills. My parents also agreed that I could continue participating in the sport. Gradually my life returned to the usual course and I got my future back: my hope and dreams returned. However, my anxiety remained at a higher level than before. I was always worried that another spot of baldness would appear and that someone would notice the already existing spots. My life had changed forever.

During my school years, I got used to the reality, in which nobody was able to disclose the name of my disease and reasons for it. As I grew up, I made no efforts to find answers to the questions I had regarding my health issue. I became accustomed to my incapacity to change something. It seemed that my hair lived its own life. It fell out and grew back whenever and wherever it wanted. I was helpless in this matter. My baldness never was severe in my childhood. It started to progress when I was around 24 years old. Because bald spots grew bigger and bigger, it became impossible to avoid this issue. Thanks to the internet, I found a lot of new information and discovered that I am not alone. It turned out that this health problem has a name - alopecia and affects many people. I decided to visit a doctor again, hoping to get some answers. Finally, after twelve long years, I was diagnosed with alopecia.

Although I finally knew what was happening with my body, finding the right remedy was extremely hard. I met with various doctors and underwent the treatments they offered. Nothing helped. Eventually, I stopped being tormented by injections in the scalp and discontinued my visits to doctors. I was already 29 years old and had only a small amount of hair on my head. Alopecia began to progress even more a few years before that time. The rate of hair loss was much faster than the rate of its growth. Every time I washed my head, I stared with terror at the amount of hair in my hands. I started to hate bath time. My inability to do something about losing my hair kept me fearful and drove me crazy. I could not accept that I was almost bald and could do nothing.

Hiding bald spots by hair that was left became impossible and I had to wear something. However, that solution made me feel unconfident and self-conscious most of the time. I often had thoughts about shaving my head as an alternative solution, but being terrified, I delayed any decisions. An idea of shaving my head and especially going out into the world with my new look was unbearable for a long time. I felt stuck and helpless!

Once, one of my acquaintances showed me pictures of bald women, encouraging me to shave my head. Because I had been thinking about that idea for a while and hated to cover my head with a cap or a hat in public, I finally dared to shave my hair. I asked my husband to help me because he was the person I trusted the most in that sensitive manner. He agreed to assist me, but we never discussed when we were going to realize that

Elena Muratova

plan. I avoided to take a final step and didn't initiate any conversation about that topic.

Suddenly, one evening, my husband appeared in front of me with a shaving machine in his hands.

"Let's do it," he said confidently. Before I had a chance to think, I was already in front of the mirror in a bathroom.

"Let's do it" I mumbled with hesitation and closed my eyes. Cold metal was touching my scalp, mercilessly cutting off my hair. I listened attentively to the sound of the shaving machine. Suddenly the sound stopped.

"Done" I heard my husband's voice. I didn't want to open my eyes. I didn't have the courage to look at the new me. I wanted to delay this moment, but I also realized that now or later, I had to face my new appearance. My head was already shaved and there was no turning back. Finally, I inhaled deeply summoning all my courage and exhaled opening my eyes.

Somebody very familiar, but at the same time different was staring at me from the mirror. I looked so strange! However, after examining myself with suspicious and then with curiosity, I concluded that I looked better than I expected. It turned out that the new me was pretty.

The first time out seemed very scary and exciting at the same time. I thought that everybody would point a finger at me and move away from me. After calming down my wild imagination, I went to the grocery store with my husband. When we arrived, I left the car and entered the store without knowing what to expect. Suddenly, I realized that no one was staring at me and no one was running away. At that moment, I felt tremendous relief!

Worries from hair loss, tension from the inability to change the situation – all these became insignificant. After being out a few times and meeting with my friends, I was convinced that I could enjoy my life with my new appearance. I finally began to accept myself. The situation that tortured me was resolved, and I was at peace.

However, that was only one side of my relationship with my body. As I learned, the body image includes many aspects such as bodily experiences, emotions, thoughts, and behavior related to body and appearance. Although I accepted my appearance, I still wasn't connected to my bodily sensations and mistreated my body. As a result, I had regular migraines and low back pain. To accept those weaknesses of my body was extremely hard.

In childhood, I perceived my body as strong and resilient. I could rely on it. Every year kids from my sports club underwent medical tests including special tests for athletes. I was proud that I showed good results and my body was healthy and strong. In the unstable situations and stressful moments, my body was one of the few things I could control and rely on. It couldn't be weak! I learnt to ignore any weakness and accept only strong parts of myself.

When alopecia came out to the scene the first time, I felt that my body betrayed me. The body that I could control before became uncontrollable. However, alopecia didn't affect my daily life in regard to training. I continued to train hard, enjoying my strength and energy. My body had been tolerating my harsh attitude not for a year, not for two years, but for twenty years. It gave up on me when I retired from sports.

In the past, when my former teammates, who were older and had already retired from professional sport, told me that their body felt apart after leaving sports, I couldn't believe them. It was a mystery for me: why health problems came to them not during their sports career, but after they retired. Guess what? I was able to resolve that mystery later, because it happened to me too when I quit mogul skiing.

At first, it did seem not logical. I didn't have migraines, low back pain and severe alopecia when I was involved in excessive physical activities. Then, when I became less active, I started to have health problems. However, I realized that after being under such pressure for many years, my body, finally, relaxed. Imagine that the body, metaphorically speaking, is a metal spring in your hands, which you pressed tough. The more pressure you apply, the more a spring stretches out when you release it. Because I didn't pay any attention to my body, treated it badly and pushed hard, it almost fell apart when I softened physical and mental demand. From being strong and energetic, my body went to the opposite side of a spectrum – became fragile and exhausted.

I had to adapt to a new norm and accept my weaknesses. It took a long time to adjust to all changes. For instance, for months, I continued to do exercises in a gym that hurt my back. The idea of not doing them simply didn't cross my mind. After some period of time, I gradually became aware that I could substitute those exercises with something more beneficial to me. However, at the beginning, I couldn't accept my weakness – my inability to do specific movements because of the low back pain. For me to accept that situation was to acknowledge my age, changes in my body, lost skills, and my limitations.

Being energetic, I often pushed through my symptoms of exhaustion that caused a migraine. Because I wasn't able to slow down my hectic lifestyle, my body did it for me. When I had a severe migraine, I could do nothing. I couldn't move around or eat for hours. I was only able to lie in a dark room. For a year or even more, I went to work with an incipient or in some cases with a strong migraine. As a result, after a while, I vomited and felt terrible.

At some point I couldn't ignore signals from my body anymore, because they were too strong. That is why I started to make small steps towards improvements of my lifestyle, so I could feel better physically and mentally. For me, this challenging but beneficial journey is reflected in two words – self-love and self-care.

CHAPTER 6
SELF-LOVE. WHAT THE HECK IS IT?

In the past, self-love and self-care were mixed in one for me. Basically, to love myself meant to care about myself mostly by sleeping well, eating healthy, having an occasional massage or buying something new.

That narrow view expanded with time. I realized that self-love is not only about self-care. For example, self-love is also about accepting all my emotions. It was so easy to love myself when I achieved success or felt great. However, when I made a mistake, experienced unpleasant painful feelings or met with dark parts, I couldn't love myself. I perceived myself as a bad person when I felt anger, envy, fear and so on.

In my childhood, I dreamt of turning off all unpleasant feelings and be a better version of myself. My mom's friend portrayed the ideal woman. My imagination finished her image by adding a few more characteristics, creating a superwoman. This ideal superwoman was so strong and imperturbable. Nothing could disturb her, and the face was calm under any circumstances. Her movements were well-coordinated and confident. Every gesture manifested impregnability and adamant willpower.

"Oh, she certainly keeps everything under control," I

thought with admiration. "I wish I was like her. Why am I so sensitive?" Nobody liked it when I was upset or crying. It seemed that in my parental family, I was more sensitive than other family members. I wished I was cold-blooded and didn't feel emotional pain, because it seemed like the only way to a happy life. However, despite all my efforts to suppress my unpleasant feelings, they still appeared.

Many years later, I understood that it is incorrect to divide feelings into good and bad categories. All feelings play a crucial role in our life. If I suppress "negative" feelings, not experience them, not letting them be, I can't experience the other uplifting part of the feelings like happiness, satisfaction and so on. After many years of futile efforts to be iron-strong, I realized that I wasn't actually living, like some part of me was dead. How can you be alive and enjoy life in full if you are not truly you, if you are partial?

For me, feelings play the same role as the lamps on my car's dashboard. They are not bad or good. They just reflect my current condition. Green lights are pleasant feelings. Yellow and red lights are unpleasant feelings of different intensity. Green lights signal that everything is going well in my environment. I can relax and focus on whatever I am doing. Yellow lights notify me that there is a minor issue. Red lights show that something requires my immediate attention. For example, irritation can signal that somebody doesn't respect my personal boundaries. Anger, more intense irritation, can indicate that I am under too much pressure because of the deadline. I can ignore these signals; however, it will most likely lead to more harmful consequences such as depression or severe migraines.

Emotions simply show me that I need to pay attention to a specific aspect of my life and work towards a resolution. Although it still can be hard, I do my best to pay attention to all signals from my soul. I think true self-love is not only about buying new things or having other treats. True self-love includes acceptance of unpleasant feelings and meeting with suppressed emotions.

Meeting with my anger and being able to tolerate others' anger was one of the most difficult parts of that way to self-love. As I mentioned in the previous chapters, in my childhood, I didn't have a healthy model of relationships with anger. There were two opposite ways to deal with this emotion: to express destructive anger or to be very pleasing, showing only passive aggression from time to time.

I always followed the second way. Because anger is crucial for healthy strong personal boundaries, I struggled with the protection of my boundaries – physical and psychological. Firstly, without recognizing my frustration and irritation, I couldn't determine my boundaries and didn't know what was normal and what wasn't appropriate. As a result, many people could easily violate my boundaries. I just stayed silent in a situation when I should defend myself. For instance, I allowed other people to be rude to me, take my things or touch me when I didn't like it.

Secondly, neither I knew how to show my anger nor how to deal with others' aggression in its various forms. I felt extremely uncomfortable and even scared when somebody close to me was angry. I also right away experienced guilt even if my actions aren't the cause of the person's emotional state. My response was to settle the situation or escape it. To confront others even about something minor was often extremely hard. Recently, I realized that I had a habit of substituting anger with tears. If anger was addressed towards me, I would rather cry than be assertive.

The worse thing about suppressing my anger was that I wasn't able to declare my wishes. I kept most of my wishes to myself and wasn't able to bring self-care in my life. I felt upset and frustrated in many moments. To say about my desires aloud meant to meet with my own irritation or anger and express myself, causing inconvenience to another person. It was very different from my usual pattern of giving in or avoiding. Only after connecting with the energy of anger, I was able to put myself first and openly talk with others about what I wanted which is another dimension of self-love.

It took me time to change my behavior patterns, feel more empowered and confront others. For example, after beginning life with my husband, months passed before I expressed my concern about cheese in our fridge. I hate it that after cheese is open and not put back into the fridge properly covered, it became hard. I always wrap the cheese after cutting off some slices. Because my husband didn't have this habit, I often found out that the cheese was dried out.

The first step on the way to expressing my wish was to sense my irritation. It arose every time I was cutting hard cheese slices, but I simply didn't notice it at first. The second step required me to share my feelings with my husband. Wow, I couldn't dare to take this step for some time because I was afraid of him becoming sad and rejecting me.

"This is just a piece of cheese!" I tried to calm myself down. However, my imagination showed a picture of me being in despair and loneliness.

"All these bad things happen when you express your desires and claim yourself." The fear concluded, adding fuel to my fears.

Once, I understood that not sharing my feelings and concerns with my husband could lead to arguing. For sure, one day, all suppressed irritations would break out, creating a hard time for us. I didn't want that scenario for our relationships, so I was brave enough to talk to my husband about the cheese situation. I expressed how irritated and frustrated I was. I tried to remember the advice I once heard: "When you are dissatisfied with a person use I-statements instead of blaming her or him." Luckily, I was able to express myself in that way, and my husband took it well. He didn't leave me because of the cheese. I am smiling right now thinking about those moments, because it looks insignificant. However, the feelings were almost overpowering at that time.

Finally, the third step, which I took right after sharing my feelings, involved expressing my wish to keep that cheese wrapped, so it doesn't get hard.

"Yes, no problem." my husband replied. "I didn't know it

was so important for you."

I began with the small wishes and needs similar to the story about the cheese. Gradually my courage grew, and I was able to reveal my more significant desires. That process made me more confident, resilient and empowered.

Even though I could declare some of my needs in the past, I still was lacking emotional resources to satisfy them. My tendency to care about others more than myself also was an obstacle. The situation with the bed is a perfect example. When we moved to Victoria, BC, we didn't have any furniture. We rented an unfurnished apartment and were going to obtain the things we needed gradually. Slowly we bought chairs and a dining table, work desks and a dresser, but we were still sleeping on the floor.

I was constantly thinking about buying a used mattress and a bed. However, the thing was that my husband is tall and doesn't like to sleep on a short bed. I wanted to buy a long used mattress, but I couldn't find any for sale. My husband's comfort was in the first place, which stopped me from buying a short mattress. We also didn't have extra money, so we couldn't order a long, handcrafted mattress and bed.

My husband didn't complain about sleeping on the floor and also agreed to sleep on a short mattress. However, even his words weren't able to change my perception of the situation. I was still worried that he would experience discomfort. It took me over two years to finally put my own feelings first. In the beginning, we bought a short mattress and a box spring. It was short for my husband but perfect for my height. Finally, I cared not only about others but also about myself. After a while, we purchased a long handcrafted mattress and built a custom bed frame. That bed became a symbol of self-care for me. Every time I laid down on it, I felt satisfied and loved. I sensed my right to realize my wishes.

When my husband Ivan was studying and I was building my business from scratch, we didn't have enough income. Our savings mostly were spent on Ivan's education as an international student and necessary living expenses. At the same time, my relatives owned me a significant amount of money. I wanted to get them back but felt guilty about initiating a conversation with my relatives about the money they owed me.

Before leaving Russia, I lent money to my sister to buy a car without setting up a payment plan to return the money. I offered her this money, so she didn't have to borrow it from a bank and pay interest. She promised to return the borrowed amount back. Time passed, I moved to Canada, but there was no clarity about a deadline for paying back. I didn't dare to start the conversation, because I was hoping for her financial situation to improve first. She never began the conversation to return the money either. During that time, she got married. I thought that it wasn't the right time to talk about money. Then she had a child. Their financial situation became even farther away from the ideal one. Again, I thought that her need for money was greater than my own.

A similar situation occurred with my parents. I gave away to them my apartment, which I had bought some years ago in my native town. They were earning money from renting it out. It was challenging to ask them to give back the money I invested. I just briefly discussed this topic without emphasis on essential details.

After talking about these situations with my counsellor, I realized that I not only felt irritated, I also felt guilty and anxiety-ridden about claiming my money back. In addition, I finally recognized that my parents and sister had a better living condition than me. They had cars and furniture in their apartments. At the same time, I didn't have a bed and was living in a different country! Anger gave me energy and strength for an unpleasant conversation, which before I postponed for many months.

Before, I perceived anger only as a bad emotion. Now I understand that anger is very helpful. I once asked an acquainted who was a counsellor if she is aware of any groups for working with anger. Her immediate response was connected to groups that help to control anger. It wasn't something I expected to hear, because I mastered that skill already. I didn't need to control my anger; I wanted to learn how to let it be more in my life. Fortunately, with time I found out that there are healthy ways to express my aggression in a safe way. When I stopped seeing only polarities of this emotion: constant pleasing and giving in or damaging rage, I began to embrace the positive energy of anger. It made me more resilient and helped me to care about myself much more than I did before.

For me, self-love also means to value my needs as high or sometimes even higher than the needs of my family members or other people. In the end, I can't support others if I am depleted and broken. However, in the past, I struggled with valuing myself as much as others. Starting in my childhood, my over-caring attitude towards my parents took new forms when I began to earn more money. I remember one time I paid for the new windows for their condo, so they can initiate renovation. Then, when my mom had her fiftieth birthday, I and my sister paid for my parent's trip to Europe. It was my mom's dream to visit Prague. My initial idea was to organize for them a trip to Prague, but then I extended an itinerary by including car rental and a trip to Austria. They had an unforgettable vacation and I was proud of myself.

Because of my low self-worth, I always felt fantastic satisfying the needs of others but felt guilty doing something for myself. This guilt was located deeply inside me and I didn't know how to get rid of it. I sensed that I didn't deserve to think about myself. The strategy of focusing on others and making them happy but not myself was my coping mechanism in my childhood. To the time I grew up, it became my trait, part of me. When I did something for myself, deep inside, I felt guilty because I wasn't worthy enough to put myself first.

In many situations in the past, my feelings and actions weren't recognized as valuable and also led to rejection, so I began truly to believe that I was an insignificant person. That is why, in order to please others and not to feel abandoned, I tried to do as little for myself as possible. I also avoided asking people close to me for help or support and tried to rely only on myself. My belief that I had no right for help, my needs and self-care were formed.

Many years later, I realized that I deserve to have desires and satisfy them. Protection of my personal boundaries; acceptance of my anger, guilt, and fear; more focus on myself - all these increased my self-worth. I began to value myself as much as other people that were reflected in my actions. For instance, after getting a bed in our apartment, I continued to create a comfortable living space for myself. I got rid of all the uncomfortable shoes and clothes I had. It also became much easier to accept presents and help from others. In addition, I made some improvements in my lifestyle. I became more mindful about my physical symptoms of fatigue and allowed myself to rest more than usual. I stopped to eat dark chocolate and taking caffeinated drinks because I didn't feel good after. It helped to prevent migraines.

I began to have more time for myself over the weekend and say no to my husband's offers if I wanted something different. It was hard to do because I felt uneasy and guilty. It also was strange for me to go somewhere alone without Ivan. However, I knew that those feelings would pass and instead, I would feel satisfied from realizing my desires. Eventually, I learnt not only to express my desires but also began to have enough inner strength to realize them.

Because for so many years, I suppressed my needs, I now sometimes feel overwhelmed by choices around me. The realization that I can do, try, learn, have, and experience various things knocks me down because for so many years, I didn't have that opportunity in my life. I am also afraid of losing all these opportunities. It still seems that if I can't get something right away, there will be no such possibility in the future. It makes me very anxious. It is still difficult to believe that nobody can take away this my right to fulfill my desires and feeling of self-worth.

Acceptance of my femininity was also a part of getting back to self-love. I had a hard time with that acceptance because the message about femininity and appearance that I received from various sources such as family members, social media, and friends often weren't in line with my own views. When I was a teenager, I had no idea what way to follow. Social media depicted a woman as somebody who every day has makeup, polishes nails, wears high heels and dresses, and applies many skincare products. My mom represented an almost opposite way of being a woman. She rarely dressed up and rarely wore dresses and skirts. To be honest, the weather in my native town was a huge obstacle to dressing up. When it is cold, windy and every sidewalk hidden by thick layer of snow, most people prefer to be in warm pants and winter boots. When I was a little child, I wore dresses in childcare. Then the older I became, the more I shifted to pants. Dresses entered my life again when I became an adult and moved to a warmer climate.

Having wide shoulders, small breast size and athletic bodybuild, I didn't feel womanly enough. I tried to follow the model of femininity portrayed by social media. I bought products for makeup, shoes with high heels, and face creams. However, after a short time, I became tired of all those rituals and stopped using them. Makeup products and face creams expired, nail polish dried up, and high heels were covered by dust in a closet.

I had the idea that having long hair made me look more womanly. That is why, when my hair fell out, I lost this connection with my femininity. On one hand, it was a harsh experience, but on another hand, I finally had to make a revision of my beliefs about how a woman should look and behave.

Around that time, I took an online course with a fashion stylist. I already had experience with hiring a fashion stylist in Russia. That lady told me what type of body I have, what styles suit me and what I should wear. Expecting something like this from an online course, I started my first task with incredulity. However, the approach of that stylist was different. The first task was to go through various fashion pictures on Pinterest and choose the one that I liked without thinking if this style suits me or not. I followed the instruction and created a folder with all the pictures that got my attention. It turned out that the pictures I chose represented my style in clothing. The next step, the most valuable for me, was to share my folder with other participants and have a look at their collections. I was shocked to see how different each selection of fashion pictures was from each other. I realized that everybody had her own unique style. Even though some styles were very alien to me, they were personalized.

This experience helped me to see that it is not necessary to follow some specific standards to be stylish. I applied this approach to femininity and realized that everybody's femininity is unique. That realization gave me the freedom to accept my own way to experience femininity without make-up, high heels and hair. I was able to accept myself and my body because I didn't need to follow any narrow social media standards anymore.

Another way to self-love was to create a healing, supportive environment around me. Being in sport for so many years, I became used to the fact that I couldn't choose my environment. During training camps, I didn't have a lot of choices with whom to live or train. I was far from the idea that I can change my environment and make it more comfortable. I always thought that my only option was to adjust. When I retired from sports, I continued to live up to that norm. I am talking not only about living space but in general about people around, about work environment and so on.

When I moved to Victoria, I got a job in one of the fitness centres. I struggled there since the first day because the environment was stressful and unpleasant for me. One month passed by, but I still worked there. On my way home in the evenings I cried because I didn't want to go there the next day. The pivotal moment was when I started to notice the option for changing that situation. Although it was hard, I decided to quit. I felt so relieved but more important that I sensed my ability to make my environment comfortable. This completed my journey to self-love, at least one part of it because I am still in a process.

CHAPTER 7
WITHIN LIMITS AND BEYOND

I had a mixed relationship with limitations in my life. On one hand, I hated many rules forced upon me from outside. For example, when I attended childcare, I always was frustrated by the fact that I needed to have a nap in the afternoon. Some rules at my grandparents' house irritated me a lot. On the other hand, I unconsciously created limiting beliefs and ideas in my mind. For instance, I thought that sport is the only way to satisfaction and self-realization. I also had many "shoulds" in my head: how a woman should look and behave, what romantic relationship should be, what way I should feel and so on. Only after working with a counsellor I started to notice how narrow my vision to various areas of my life was.

However, in any way, it was challenging for me to see my limitations. Growing up, I believed that I could control everything and didn't see my limits on it. I was sure that I could make my parents happy or unhappy, control my emotions and my life. I felt responsibility and guilt if some bad events happened to me or somebody I cared about. I was thinking that my thoughts and feelings led to those events or I did not try hard enough to prevent bad things from happening. I was extremely afraid of facing reality where I had limitations and couldn't control many things in my life. This thought scared the hell out of me. For many years I followed that pattern of not meeting and not accepting my limits. As often as possible, I completely ignored their existence. Because of that, I pushed myself too hard, freaked out when I was losing control, was in constant tension and couldn't see many situations realistically.

For a long time, I refused to see the limits of the past. For example, I couldn't accept my childhood the way it was. I still had an unconscious desire to change it, to satisfy all my childish needs. One day I was writing a letter to my dad without any intention to send it to him. I did it as an exercise to heal my traumas. It was a very insightful process for me! For the first time, I realized that at twenty-nine years of age, I still expected to get from my dad what I didn't in my childhood. With tears running down my cheeks, I was writing about different painful events and about what I missed in our relationships. I became aware that I still wanted him to play with me, read me books, go for a walk, hug me often and be compassionate. This little me inside desired so strongly to fulfill her childish needs. I was crying because I realized my limitations in satisfying those needs. For the first time in my life, I not only became aware of my hidden expectations but also about the fact that my childhood couldn't be changed. It happened; I can't relive it. I couldn't be the five years old girl again and my dad couldn't be the age he was at that time. The only way to deal with it was to accept that my childhood is unchangeable and to stop waiting for something that would never happen.

This understanding helped me to focus on my current relationship with my dad. I was able to see him with the eyes of a twenty-nine years old woman, not a five years old girl. My dad and I were finally able to be on the same level. Still father and daughter, but also two adults who now have needs and expectations that are different from the past ones. It created more space inside me for pleasant memories and accepting him the way he is.

In a romantic relationship, I also ignored some limitations for years. I didn't want to see that my partner couldn't completely satisfy my needs in acceptance, love and confidence. To be honest, I was too demanding, clingy, and fragile. That is why many of my romantic relationships in the past had an unhealthy pattern. When I was able to finally see an inability of the romantic relationship to give me what I needed, I realized that I was looking in the wrong direction. Acceptance of this type of limitation helped me to take responsibility for my needs and turn towards myself. Since that time, I knew that my huge need to be loved would be satisfied when I begin to fully accept and love myself.

Money is another limit that disturbed me a lot. It seemed that having more money would give me more freedom and I would be able to do whatever I wish. Sweet dreams! It is another manifestation of my desire not to have any limits. With time I realized that having a lot of money will not erase limitations from my life completely. Such limits as time and unpredictability will always be with me.

Another thing I struggled to accept was the limits of my energy and body functions. As you know from previous chapters, I didn't notice my physical limitations such as pain and fatigue for a long time. As a result, I had migraines and back pain. When I was an athlete, I also didn't want to accept that I couldn't learn new skills fast enough or constantly be at my best physical condition. It affected a lot of my decisions in my sports career. Instead of focusing on something that I could improve in the given time frames, I put a lot of effort into learning new jumps that required much more time that I had. I was so stubborn in proving myself that there were no limits.

When I retired from sports, I continued to live as if I had endless energy. I didn't give myself a break when I felt tired. I planned too many things to do and then felt frustrated if I was exhausted. When I just started my business, I didn't have many clients. I decided to take a part-time job in one of the fitness studios. It was a group trainer position that required me to be at the studio at 5.45 am a few days a week. Sometimes I needed to cover somebody's shift and came there on additional days. The problem was that I lived far away and didn't have a car. To get to the studio, I biked for 50 minutes because there were no buses at that early time. I had to leave home before 5 am, and I am not an early morning person at all! As a result, I created a lot of stress for my body. I didn't feel well but continued to push myself.

I didn't want to face my physical limitations until I started to have severe migraines. I can't express how difficult it was to come to terms with limited amount of energy and physical resources. It turned out I am not a Super Woman and my body has its limits. It also was a reminder that my body changes with time. It will never be the same as it was ten years ago. It will continue to change because aging is inevitable. I can't push it as hard as I did in the past. Even though I have a positive example of how my parents are facing aging, it's still tricky to accept the fact that I can't have my body at its best condition forever.

The first time I realized with sadness that some changes in my body couldn't be reversed was when I had my first knee surgery. On the day of the ACL (anterior cruciate ligament) replacement surgery, I was looking at my right knee. I tried to print in my memory that smooth skin without a scar which was going to appear there in a few hours. I remember thinking: "It will never be the same." It was a new type of thought for me. In the past, especially when I was a child, I was glad to see changes in my body because they indicated my growth. I was looking forward to growing up. However, during my days in a hospital for the first time, I was scared of permanent changes in my body. I didn't want them to happen anymore.

Living within all these limits was hard. It seemed that they prevented me from living my life the way I wanted and from being happy. I never rebelled but was always curious about finding solutions to feel less limited. I expected that some new activity or action would magically help me to break free and feel happier. In my childhood, I tried different activities that were described in the books I found at home. For some time, I slept without the pillow but with a handmade device similar to a small half foam roll. I put it under my neck when I went to sleep. Once, I found a book about one of the approaches in martial arts. For a while, I practiced some of the exercises that were described there. It seems like I always was looking for something that would change my life for the better and make me happier.

Fortunately, with time my perception of the limitations changed. I learnt that I always have freedom, even within limits. I can always choose my attitude to any situation or to a limit I face. For instance, I can't change my baldness, but I can choose my attitude. I can feel insecure and self-conscious about my baldness or I can embrace it and turn it into my uniqueness. I can fight my migraine and push through it or I can notice the triggers and accept that I need to slow down and have more rest.

However, to choose freedom is a challenge because I have to accept my responsibility for my choices. Freedom and responsibility come together. I am free only when I feel responsible for my life. It is impossible to be free when I give responsibility for my life to somebody else; when I blame somebody for my choices, feelings, loneliness, my unsatisfied needs and so on. Only when I accept my responsibility, I can feel empowered, able and in charge of my life. It is all about a personal choice. If someone chooses not to be responsible, he or she chooses to refuse freedom. I also try to remember that I always make a choice even if I choose not to make a choice. I make a decision to stay passive and not to choose. However, in this case, most likely, somebody will decide for me and not necessary in my advantage.

Making a choice is hard because every time I choose something, I sacrifice something else. Having so many interests, I constantly had to pick only a few from many options because my time is limited. There are only 24 hours in a day, and I can't fit everything I want into those limits. Every time making a choice, I had to let other options go. How to focus on only one option when there are so many of them around, especially when they all attractive? In addition, life choices always force me to face limits in a more global way. I have to meet with the fact that I am mortal.

To be honest, by avoiding my other limitations, in reality, I try to avoid the biggest and scariest limitation of my life – my death. Sometimes facing this limitation causes me to have a sort of panic attack. When it happens, I feel not a fear of dying but unbearable horror and experience something similar to derealization. My heart rate goes up, my breathing becomes hyperventilated. My entire body is in a panic mode and I can't be immobile.

This panic attack happened for the first time when I was around twelve years old. I was in a bathroom, taking a shower. Suddenly the horror seized me. I quickly put my clothes on and ran out of the bathroom. Breathing heavenly and shacking, I was walking back and forward in front of the entrance to the living room where my mom was. In a short time, the horror stepped away as fast as it seized me. I was confused and didn't know what to do.

"Is everything all right?" My mom noticed me and asked.

"Yes." I replied without hesitation.

Since that time, I had these panic attacks regularly. Sometimes they happened every month, sometimes just once per year. However, it always attacks me when I am alone, especially when I am in bed in the evening. I never talked about them with anybody until recent times. I just assumed that fear of death in this extreme manifestation was a normal part of human life. The only thing that helped me to avoid that horror was to distract myself by engaging my mind in any activity. When I felt that the horror was coming, I started to read a book, to immerse myself in the social media or to play a card game "Spider" on my cell phone.

Once I was listening to a radio program run by a psychologist. He and his listeners were talking about various things. My attention was fully in when they started to discuss the topic of death. For the first time, I realized that maybe my horror was not normal. I got hope that life without it was possible. It took me five years to decrease the intensity and frequency of those panic attacks. That was possible because I began to explore my anxiety instead of suppressing it.

CHAPTER 8
BOLDNESS TO LIVE

Anxiety is my eternal companion. It is always with me. Even if it is not in my focus, it is somewhere in the background. I try to keep myself busy because if I slow down, anxiety becomes more intense. That is why relaxation is an extremely hard thing for me. I simply can't be with myself one on one. I feel very uncomfortable and uneasy when I have to meet with myself if there is nothing to do. My husband Ivan can walk alone without listening to music and without any purpose for a long time. I can't. Even the idea of this option scared me in the past.

I can't remember when anxiety became permanent in my life. Since childhood, I had always been an anxious person. Of course, the challenges I had in my childhood contributed to it. Maybe the biggest contributor was my fear of being vulnerable. Experiencing this fear, I had to control everything in order to avoid moments of vulnerability. The moments of my weakness were totally unbearable for my childish mind. For instance, when I was bullied, rejected, made fun of or completely lonely in harsh situations, I often felt sharp stinging emotional pain. I had no idea how to make that pain fade away. The only solution that came to my mind was to have total control over everything, which made me feel strong — losing control meant to be vulnerable and, as a result, weak. However, despite my effort I never could have enough control because life is unpredictable and uncontrollable by nature. All the time, the sense of control was slipping away from me. I put a lot of effort into catching control in the last moment and nervously keeping it in my hands. The more I tried to control my life and my future, the more anxious I became. I constantly scanned my parents' and other people's mood. It gave me an opportunity to react in time if I needed to bring a situation back to balance. I tried to make other people happy because it prevented painful situations from happening. In addition, all the time I monitored and controlled my own behavior and action which killed my spontaneity.

It was also difficult for me to trust that everything would be okay. That lack of trust boosted my anxiety. My catastrophic thinking created in my mind pictures of the worst-case scenarios. When I was around eight years old, my parents, my sister and I went to a summer training camp with many other coaches and athletes. At that time, my dad still had problems with alcohol. My parents argued while we were there. I remember our room with old furniture on the second floor of the two-story motel style building. One evening after my parents argued my father left. I heard some discussion that adults including my mom had right after. Something they said made me think that my dad took a rope and went to commit suicide. My imagination went wild depicting me all horror of not seeing him again. I couldn't find a place for myself. The worst thing was that I could do nothing. I wanted to find my dad and save him, but I had no idea where he went. Time almost stopped and arrows of the clock moved very slowly, shuddering during every move. I was on edge during all those hours of waiting. Finally, my dad came back. He was alive! He was back! Nothing else was more important to me at that moment.
      Probably, I got my catastrophic thinking from my paternal grandmother. She was an extremely anxious person

because she always expected that something bad was going to happen. I can't imagine how she managed to worry about everybody in the extended family. Every evening before going to bed she prayed for her husband, each of her kids, grandkids and other members of the family. I found that ritual strange when I was a kid. Only when she died, I realized how meaningful her daily prays were. The simple knowledge that every day she thought about me and wished me the best in the world was extremely supportive. With her death, I lost such valuable support which I even didn't recognize while she was alive.

The catastrophic thinking limited my life a lot. I couldn't trust the world. If my coach or boss wanted to talk to me, I right away expected negative comments from them. If I saw an unexpected call from somebody I know, I was afraid to hear bad or unpleasant news. My issues with trust raised my anxiety level. For example, if Ivan wasn't home on time, I started to worry. In my head I saw all the negative pictures of a car accident or other bad things. This anxiety quickly became very strong and I couldn't refrain from calling Ivan. It always turned out that he went to a grocery store or went for a drink with his friends after acting class. Only when was I assured that everything was ok with him, I was able to relax. Maybe these situations with Ivan reminded me of some situations in my childhood. When I was a child and my father wasn't home from work, I started to panic. His absence meant that he probably was drinking with his friends. I was extremely worried that something bad could happen to him. Maybe he could be robbed, made fun of or hit by a car. It was always a relief to see him back even though I also felt angry and frustrated that he was drunk.

In addition to the fear of being vulnerable and to catastrophic thinking, I also had another contributor to my anxiety – a belief that I needed to make maximum efforts to get something. For many years I wasn't aware of that unhelpful belief. I just knew that I had to push myself to the extreme level for receiving something from life. That unconscious belief affected many areas of my life. I had to put a huge amount of effort into romantic relationships to occasionally feel loved. I expected that I couldn't be loved just for being myself but that I had to earn a good attitude from others towards me. When I was an athlete, I believed that I had to do more than other athletes to achieve sports success. It seemed that it was easier for others to reach bigger goals even if they didn't put as much efforts as I did. No matter in what area of life but it always seemed that other people got more by doing less.

My relationships with money also reflected that belief. I thought that only by working excessively I will get money. Money was associated with a lot of tension and stress. Firstly, in my childhood, I saw how my parents struggled to make ends meet. A few summers my dad worked during his vacation in a construction company repairing roofs because the salary of a coach wasn't enough for living. Secondly, I had my own unpleasant experience with money. When I went to my first competitions abroad in 1996, I was shocked by the abundance of food, clothes and other things. I was ten years old and other athletes were older than me. It is challenging to accept today, but I stole a few things from the stores. I saw that other kids did it and tried it too. The interesting fact is that for myself I stole a cheap pack of juice, but I took more expensive things for my family: a dog leash for our dog and a ski scraper for my dad. Initially, I experienced just some discomfort because I knew stealing was a bad idea, but later when my dad used that ski scrapper, I felt very guilty every time. I didn't want to steal again.

When I was twelve years old and went for that dramatic trip to Italy, my father gave me some money in Italian liras. He also asked me to buy a ski poles for my sister. Being a child and missing my home, I called my parents a few times from Italy by stationary phone that cost me some money. Then, I also bought myself a few ice creams and maybe some other sweets. Of course, I bought a beautiful ski poles for my dear sister. At the end of the trip, I had no money left. When I came home, it turned out that I had to bring some money back. My father also was angry that the ski poles were too short. I felt guilty and scared. He asked for the rest of the money; I couldn't find a better solution than to say that somebody stole them. I was too afraid to say the truth. However, the situation became worse when he mentioned his intention to call the coach I was with at that trip and bring this situation up. I freaked out because I knew I was lying. Fortunately, I didn't have another conversation with my dad about that trip. I don't know if he called that coach or not, but he didn't initiate another conversation.

The same year or maybe a year later, my parents decided to send my sister and me to my grandparents for a vacation a few weeks before the end of the school year. Usually, we left right after the last day of school. The thing was that train tickets for kids were cheaper during the school year and my parents decided to save some money. The way to Moscow would take two nights and one day on a train. Then one of their friends was going to meet us in Moscow in the morning and took care of us before our next train in the evening. The train from Moscow to my grandparent's place would take five hours. Everything was fine at first. We packed up our bags and left to a train station feeling very excited. However, it turned out that my parents left the necessary documents from our school at home. Those documents were proof that we were allowed to have our low-priced tickets. A trainwoman didn't want to let us on board. My parents were frustrated and tried to negotiate with the trainwoman. She was reluctant at first but then allowed my sister and me to take that train with the condition that I would pay the difference in ticket price during the trip. My parents agreed and gave me the necessary amount of money. When the train left the station, I was shaking inside. The entire situation was extremely stressful for me. It was my first trip to my grandparents without adults and with the responsibility of my sister who was around eight years old at that time. Now I also had to deal with money. When the train started to move, I was still afraid that we could be disembarked at the next train station. Being in my worries, I went through many train cars to pay that money to the leader of a train team and returned to my sister. When we stopped at the next station, nobody forced us to leave and I was able to exhale.

All those and other situations in my childhood that were connected to money influenced my attitude towards it. I began to associate money with stress, exhaustion and guilt. It is not a surprise that later in my life, I struggled with getting enough money and enjoying them. My belief that I had to push myself at work to extremes to earn money and painful emotions associated with them elevated my anxiety level.

My perfectionism made me an anxious person too. Because in the past to make mistakes was equal to losing acceptance and good attitude from my family members, I freaked out every time mistake occurred. As much as I could, I tried to avoid them. Unfortunately, there were many opportunities for doing something wrong in sport, in household tasks, in relationships and in my decision making. I spent extra time checking if my actions or tasks were correct. With time I became afraid of mistakes in general, not only of those that could affect my close relationships. I wanted to appear perfect. Every mistake and every flaw also showed me that I was vulnerable, which became similar to being weak. Those moments were unbearable.

Fortunately, with time I realized that as an adult, I could survive a situation when I am vulnerable. Now I am strong enough and have enough support to be in my vulnerability: make mistakes, have flaws and be real. All these will not destroy me anymore. I also discovered that something that I perceived as weakness is just a reality – the way things are in present moment. For example, if I am scared, tired, overwhelmed, or helpless, it doesn't mean that I am weak. It means that in a certain moment I feel a certain way. It simply shows that this is what happening in my reality. This new attitude towards "my weakness" helped me to accept my right not be perfect all the time. This understanding gives me so much resources and energy for trying new things, for doing something challenging, and for being real in relationships.

However, I must confess that I needed my anxiety. Tension and stress caused by anxiety were beneficial for me. Firstly, when I was in a stressful situation, I could actually do the actions I needed to do. The thing is that when there was enough time and I was relaxed, I could easily go into unhelpful thinking such as, for example, being worried about what other people may think, being afraid of making mistakes or feel unconfident. However, when I was in a rush and in tension, there was no time for unhelpful thoughts, but only for a narrow focus on a task or activity. As a result, I could make a challenging phone call, express myself, or make a difficult decision. The actions that seemed very challenging when I was relaxed became doable under tension and anxiety. Fear, shyness, worries disappeared in the moments of stress and I could act in a better way.

Secondly, achieving something under pressure gave me a sense of accomplishment. I felt awesome and uplifted because I was able to make that last effort and accomplish something no matter how small or big. This attitude to my life allowed me to feel self-worth because I was thinking: "I did it! I am so damn cool!" Unfortunately, I didn't experience that uplifting feeling when I did the same things in a relaxed way. I needed this challenge to feel worthy and accomplished.

Thirdly, stress, tension and constant worries prevented me from being one on one with myself. I simply didn't have time or energy to meet with my deeper challenges, inner conflicts, or fears, including the fear of death. As I describe before, I had to focus on my romantic partner excessively for overcoming my fears in sport, tolerate painful situations, and maintain my hope. The same situation was with my stress and tension. I had to keep my stress level high constantly for not meeting with hard questions, limitations, fears and inner pain.

Being in stress all the time became the only way to live for me. I learnt how to create tension in my life without any help from others. For instance, if I needed to be somewhere, I stayed at home till the last minute and then was in a rush to get there on time. Initially, I didn't notice that I myself created that tension. Usually when it was time to leave, I simply thought that I still had enough time to change my clothes and prepare things I wanted to take with me. At the same time, all of a sudden, checking my emails, confirming some information, or washing dishes became extremely important. I simply couldn't postpone those activities till later time. My perspective of time became distorted. Only after a while, I suddenly realized that time passed by, and I was already five minutes behind my schedule. The phrase which I remember from one of the Russian movies from my childhood became a slogan of this my behaviour pattern. It says, "It is too early. It is still early. It is already late."

It is still extremely hard for me to change this pattern and not to create tension. I find it challenging to detect my unhelpful thoughts and act differently. Sometimes I can manage my time better, but in some situations, I am still in a rush and late. Another example of how I created tension for myself was eating right before I needed to leave home. Maybe it started in my childhood when I had to eat very fast after school, so I could be on time for my training session. I ate my lunch and then quickly went to skiing slopes that were fifteen-twenty minutes walk away. Being an adult, I continued to re-create this pattern in my life even though it could be avoided. Again, thinking that I had plenty of time, I started to eat later and then had to run to a bus stop because I was late. As a result, I not only created tension for my mind but also for my body. Physical activity right after eating is not a good choice.

Sadly to say, but it simply felt that I didn't have the energy to do certain things when I was relaxed. However, when I was in a stress mode, I felt very energetic for doing the same things. It is like I felt alive more when I was anxious. It wouldn't be a problem if I didn't have to sacrifice many things in my life because of this. Being anxious meant that I couldn't focus on the present and meet with true Self. This anxious way to live was a good mechanism to cope with many unpleasant things especially with the fear of death. However, I also had less satisfaction in my daily life because I forgot to experience it. It was an obstacle to fulfilling life where I could be true to me. The anxiety, that hid painful feelings, controlled me, but not the other way around. My life, my choices and my actions often were led by anxiety, not by me.

Anxiety helped me to cope with the fear of death by distracting me from meeting with myself. However, paradoxically, I also couldn't overcome that fear of death because I wasn't living fully. I was scared to live: to be mindful, to express myself, to accept limitations, to build authentic relationships with others, to think about daily experiences, to stop for a moment and just be without doing something. For many years I had been turning away from the life. This attitude resulted in my extreme fear of death and in panic attacks. The first time I was able to look at death from the different perspective happened when I was reading a book written by existential psychotherapist Irvin Yalom. I realized that awareness of death and acceptance of limited time would help me to embrace my life fully.

In the past, because I couldn't face my mortality, I was able to endlessly postpone my life. I didn't bring myself in this world through creativity. I postponed following my dreams and focused on satisfying others' needs. I didn't make necessary changes. I wasn't present and missed on many experiences. I didn't do what I wanted to do. Finally, I didn't meet with myself. It was easy to postpone all these because I didn't accept that my life was limited. I thought that one day everything would change, and I would be happy. Sometime one day in the future I would start to live fully. The realization that my life has time limits helped me to finally turn towards my life. I clearly realized I don't have a second chance to live. Meeting with my death helped me to meet with my life.

When I found this meaning in death and started to embrace

my life, my panic attacks became rarer and less intense. Even though it was hard to let my anxiety go, I started to be mindful of my daily experiences by being present and by being mindful. For example, when I walked, not ran, to a bus stop, I could stop for a few minutes and just look around me. I began to notice many things I wasn't aware of before. For example, for three years, I went the same route but never noticed the beautiful flowers in a few spots on my way. Maybe I saw them, but I didn't notice them. I just passed by, being more in my head than in my body. I realized that only experiencing my life through my body, be more mindful about what I sense I can live a fulfilled life. For instance, I started to go into nature more often and pay attention to the wonderful world around me: smell flowers, touch trees, observe birds and enjoy wind or sun on my skin.

I decided to say "Yes" to my life and embrace it in every aspect. When I made that decision, I gradually started to have more boldness to live here and now: be vulnerable and make mistakes, build authentic close relationships knowing that any of them would end at some point, ask myself and others difficult questions, live in the limits and beyond them, try something new, let my anxiety go, be creative understanding that others may criticize me, satisfy my needs, and be inconvenient for others by being assertive. I became bold enough to be myself, to experience my life here and now, not postponing till then and there.

Part Two

Helpful Tools

During my way to boldness and in the process of discovering myself, I learnt many things and passed through so many experiences that helped me to enhance the quality of my life in various areas. In the second part of my book, I want to share with you some of the practical tools that I used. Although there are many exercises that you can do on your own, I also want to highlight how enormously helpful my work with a counsellor was. I started to work with her in 2014, almost right after the Olympic Games. I am not sure how I would have dealt with all the challenges I experienced without her support. The opportunity to talk openly with somebody who would never judge, give advice or hurt was extremely helpful for me during my struggles with alopecia, life transitions, adjusting to a new life in Canada, relationships and so on.

Disclaimer

The material of this book is provided only for educational and informational purposes and does not include any form of counselling, therapy, or professional advice. If expert assistance or counselling is needed, the service of a competent professional should be sought.

The author and publisher do not assume and hereby disclaim any liability to any party for any loss, damage, or disruption caused by errors or omission, whether such errors or omissions result from negligence, accident, or any other cause.

CHAPTER 9
HOW TO BECOME MORE RESILIENT

In the past, I thought that I was a resilient person. I faced many dramatic and disturbing events but kept pushing through all the odds, having success in sport and school. Was I really resilient? Yes, but in a wrong way. That resilience was possible because I sacrificed a lot, not because I knew how to support myself. I sacrificed my health because I ignored pain and discomfort. I sacrificed myself when I constantly focused on others. I sacrificed my emotional wellbeing because I suppressed my emotions and didn't have healthy relationships. It was when I became almost bald, started to have severe migraines and chronic low back pain, that I realized I needed to find other ways to be resilient. There are four ways that helped me become resilient without sacrificing my health, wellbeing, relationships and myself.

Supportive Environment

Creativity

Self-Care

Emotional Intelligence

1. Supportive Environment.

The environment in which you live plays a crucial role in your level of resilience. I focused on three main parts when I was making my environment more supportive and healing:

- **Supportive relationships with others**
- **Good relationship with yourself**
- **Comfortable space around**

Supportive relationships with others. While it is impossible to avoid tension and stress in any interpersonal relationship, it is necessary to have more positive interactions with others than negative ones. Some relationships can be improved and made more supportive, but some relationships can't. In the second case, the best solution is to distance yourself from such people and minimize interactions with them.

Living with my husband, I realized that the most important thing for a healthy supportive relationship is effective communication, which is only possible when you can understand your feelings and motives, express them and listen to other people. Another critical part of effective communication is to check if your perception of a situation reflects reality. It was a big challenge for me because I easily conclude on situations because of my past experience and me still being connected to its hurtful feelings.

For example, at the beginning when we started our life together, we went to a gym. When our daily exercise was almost finished, Ivan offered to stop by a grocery store and buy some treats.

After taking some food in a store, I went to a section with sweets, expecting Ivan would follow me. However, when I turned around, I saw him standing in line to pay for the grocery. I became very upset and frustrated; I thought that he didn't fulfill his promise about buying treats. When I approached him, he knew something was wrong, but we couldn't communicate effectively at that moment. But when we left the store, I was able to express why I was upset. In my perception, we didn't buy any treats. Ivan was surprised because he had a different perception about the situation. He thought he bought a lot of treats: meat, salami, fruits, etc. After that conversation, we learnt that our perception to similar situations could differ significantly.

Now I try to check my perception regularly before I jump into any conclusion.

Perception check (1) consists of:
1. Description of visible behavior that you observe (of course, that description can't include negative or rude comments).
2. A few explanations of that behavior.
3. Request for clarification.

For instance, in the situation with treats, I could have said the following:
"Ivan, I noticed that we didn't buy any treats. Did you change your mind while we were here or you want to buy them in another store? I am confused. Maybe there is something else?"

Exercise. To practice in checking your perception, choose a few situations in which it would be beneficial to do. Try to form a phrase you could use for perception check.

Situation One.

_____

_____

_____

Perception Check for Situation One

_____

_____

_____

_____

Situation Two.

_____

_____

_____

Perception Check for Situation Two

_____

_____

_____

_____

Good relationship with yourself. You constantly reduce your resilience if you treat yourself poorly. Most likely, you have an inner critic inside who is active when you evaluate your actions, feel something, express yourself and so on. Sometimes this critic helps you to make the right decisions or correct your behavior but sometimes it sabotages your achievements or criticizes your actions.

If the second option described above is a primary behavior of your inner critic, try to pay more attention to your thoughts. What do you say to yourself when you make a mistake, express yourself, feel a certain emotion, interact with others, dream and so on? Try to challenge that negative comments and treat yourself as you would treat somebody you truly care about. It is important to have compassion, empathy, love, and kind words for yourself.

Exercise. Write down how you usually criticize yourself. What do you say? Then transform each phrase in a positive message.

For example, I have a tendency to criticize myself for a mistake by saying something like: "How could you do it? It is so stupid." My new positive message that I try to incorporate is, "I know you feel very upset and angry at yourself, but everybody makes mistakes. It is not possible to avoid them."

1. Unhelpful Critique

_____

New positive message

_____

2. Unhelpful Critique

_____

New positive message

_____

3. Unhelpful Critique

_____

New positive message

_____

4. Unhelpful Critique

_____

New positive message

_____
.

Comfortable space around you. A pleasant comfortable work and home space boost your resilience. Often little details such as a comfortable chair or organized spices in a cupboard evoke satisfaction and make us happier.

Exercise. Make a list of what you can make more comfortable or convenient in your home and how

1._____

2._____

3._____

4._____

5._____

6._____

Make a list of what you can make more comfortable or convenient at your work and how

1._____

2._____

3._____

4._____

5._____

6._____

2. Creativity

Creativity makes a person more resilient, because it enhances wellbeing and helps to decrease stress in everyday life. For some time in the past I thought that I wasn't a creative person. I believed that to be creative, I needed to have a talent in art, dance, music and also excessive knowledge in one of those areas. Fortunately, with time I learnt that creativity is much bigger than my narrow vision.

You can be creative in different ways. Firstly, you can be open to seeing a situation from a different perspective. It gives you the opportunity of choice to make. Secondly, creativity is about bringing your individuality and uniqueness to your work, relationships, daily tasks, hobbies and so on. Thirdly, participation in creative activities such as crafting, painting, storytelling, or cooking, helps you to express yourself. It also decreases stress, replenishes resources and enables you to gain a sense of control over your life (2).

- **Be open to seeing a situation from a different perspective**
- **Bring your individuality to every area of life**
- **Participate in creative activities**

Exercise. In what areas of your life you can bring in more creativity and how?

1._____

2._____

3._____

4._____

5._____

6._____

Exercise. Write down the type of creative activities that you've ever tried.

Here are examples of creative activities: dancing, singing, coloring, drawing, painting, playing musical instrument, making photographs, sculpting, woodworking, making jewelry or stained glass, sewing, quilting, knitting, crocheting, cross-stitching, wool spinning, weaving, basketry, baking or cooking special meals, writing (in any forms), acting, gardening, etc.

_____   _____

_____   _____

_____   _____

_____   _____

Exercise. Make a list of creative activities you like to do or want to explore. Write down when and where you can do a specific creative activity and what will you need. Remember most of the activities you can do alone or with somebody, at home or at another place.

1. Creative Activity   Where and When

_____   _____

What will you need

_____

2. Creative Activity   Where and When

_____   _____

What will you need

_____

3. Creative Activity   Where and When

_____   _____

What will you need

_____

4. Creative Activity   Where and When

_____   _____

What will you need

_____

5. Creative Activity   Where and When

_____   _____

What will you need

_____

3. Self-care

Self-care includes an ability to be present (mindfulness), an ability to be assertive, and the implementation of nourishing activities in your daily life.

- **Ability to be present (mindfulness)**
- **Ability to be assertive**
- **Nourishing activities in daily life**

An ability to be present. For me to be present or mindful means to be aware of my current experiences and needs. Am I hungry? Am I cold? Do I feel tired? Do I want to talk to somebody? Only by being mindful will I understand what is happening to me and react appropriately.

I also found out that in order to be present, I need to be in a calm state. If I am too anxious, I can't be mindful of my experiences and about the environment around me. Some events that push me out of a calm state can happen often. That is why I need to know how to make my emotions less intense by regulating my autonomic nervous system.

The autonomic nervous system regulates bodily functions such as the heart rate, digestion, respiratory rate, which is closely connected to emotions. For instance, when a person is scared, heart rate and breathing increase. Thus, by changing the breathing pattern, a person can become calmer.

There are a few exercises I usually do for self-regulation for example, when my catastrophic thinking makes me extremely nervous and I can't think clearly. I also do these easy exercises when I am too scary, worried, ashamed, or when I can't fall asleep.

Breathing exercises.
(The video of this exercise is at my YouTube channel – Elena Muratova)

Option A. When your nervous system is too active: your heart rate is high, breathing is fast, and muscles are tensed. It usually happens when you are anxious, scary, angry and so on.

Breath deeply and inhale air shorter than you exhale. For example, inhale on one count, exhale on four counts.

Option B. When you are too sluggish, depressed and lacking energy, breath deeply and inhale longer than you exhale. For example, inhale on four counts, exhale on one count.

The Basic Exercise (3)
(The video of this exercise is at my YouTube channel – Elena Muratova)

Although you can do this exercise lying, seating or

standing, it is recommended to do it while lying for the first few times.

1. Interweave your fingers together and place your hands behind the back of your head.
2. While keeping your head straight, move your eyes to the right as far as it is comfortable for you. Hold your eyes in the same position for 60 sec.
3. Bring your eyes back, so you can look straight ahead.
4. Move your eyes to the left side as far as it is comfortable for you and keep them at that spot for 60 sec. Remember to keep your head straight.
5. Bring your eyes back, so you can look straight ahead.

During this exercise, you most likely will sigh, swallow or yawn that will be a sign of the relaxation and regulation of your autonomic nervous system.

An ability to be assertive. Assertiveness is the ability to express your feelings and thoughts clearly without judging or attacking another person (1). This skill helps you to protect your physical or psychological boundaries, to say "no" to unpleasant people or situations and not to force yourself to participate in activities you don't like. In other words, assertiveness is a great and necessary tool for self-care.

I actually started to talk to others instead of keeping everything inside. When I communicate with others, I use "I-statement." I describe the situation and my feelings about it without attacking others. I also share consequences that the situation could have on me or my relationship with other people and then express my intention.

For instance, when I talked to Ivan about the dried out cheese in a fridge, I used the "I-statement" (1), as shown below.
"Ivan, when you don't wrap the cheese, it hardens. I often feel very upset because I don't like to eat hard cheese. My

frustration grows every time I find dried out cheese. You probably didn't know how important it was for me. Could you please wrap the cheese after you put it back into the fridge?"

Assertive behavior doesn't guarantee you to get the outcome you want. Some people just don't want to listen or consider your point. Some people don't want to look for a compromise. In some situations, when others become too aggressive, it is better to go away or cease any relationship with such a person. However, "I-statement" gives you the best chances to effectively communicate to others your needs and thoughts in any conflict situations (small or big).

Exercise "I-statement"
Think about a situation in which you could use assertiveness. Create your I statement which should include the following parts (in any order):

o   description of a situation/behavior.
o   your interpretation of the reasons for a situation or behavior.
o   Your feelings.
o   Consequences.
o   Intention.

Situation One

_____

_____

_____

_____

_____

Situation Two

_____

_____

_____

_____

_____

I was able to become more assertive when I started to feel that I am worthy enough, learnt to tolerate other people's feelings, and also connect with my anger.

To start feeling worthy can take some time and work with past traumas. However, understanding what I sacrifice when I am not assertive was one of the steps towards self-care and self-worth.

Exercise. Write down what you sacrifice in the situations when you are not assertive.

This exercise helps to see the benefits of being assertive.

1._____

2._____

3._____

4._____

5._____

6._____

For many years, I tried to avoid any conflicts and also situations when another person experienced any unpleasant feelings. For example, I often checked if Ivan had taken his keys or wallet when he was leaving home. At that time, we shared our car and he often took a bus to get to work. I imagined that if he forgets his keys and couldn't get into home in the evening because I would be away, he would be frustrated and upset. I simply couldn't tolerate not only facing his unpleasant feelings but even a possibility that situation like that could happen. Trying to prevent Ivan from experiencing frustration and sadness, I couldn't focus on my own activities.

However, after a while, I became aware of my experience in those situations, I discovered that in reality, I couldn't tolerate my own feelings, not Ivan's. The thing is that Ivan's unpleasant feelings evoked guilt and fear of rejection in me. With astonishment, I realized that for all that time I tried to prevent myself but not Ivan from certain feelings. I started to practice to tolerate my emotions. Of course, understanding the reasons why I had such a strong emotional response made it easy to live through those emotions. I also knew from experience that emotion comes and goes, so I just needed to wait until it becomes less intense.

Exercise. Think about situations when difficulties with tolerating another person's feelings prevented you from self-care (e.g., focusing on yourself, doing something you want or not doing what you didn't want). What did you feel you couldn't tolerate?

1. Describe a situation

Describe your feelings

_____

_____

2. Describe a situation

_____

_____

Describe your feelings

_____

_____

3. Describe a situation

_____

_____

Describe your feelings

_____

_____

I was afraid of expressing my anger and mastered the skill of suppressing it. However, it prevented me from being assertive and satisfied. It was easier to give in than show that I have needs or feel angry. I perceived anger as something totally negative. With time, I learnt that anger can be positive too and that it has many forms: irritation, frustration, resentfulness, hostility, rage, etc. All of these can be beneficial in different situations. When you are in a dangerous situation, rage can help you to escape it. Irritation and frustration can signal that some of your needs are not satisfied or being met. Anger can indicate that your boundaries need protection.

I also realised that anger could give so much energy to accomplish something or make a change. It can help to start something that I have postponed for a very long time, to say "No," to take care of myself and so on.

Exercise. Write down the positive aspects of expressing anger.

1._____

2._____

3._____

4._____

5._____

6._____

In addition, I found a few tools that I can use to let my anger out that was impossible to release in a social environment in a safe and appropriate way. Here is a list:

o   Screaming in a car or in another place where others can't hear you.

o   Bed tantrum. You need to lie down on your back on a

bed and then kick repeatedly the mattress with your feet and hands as hard as you can. Continue until you are out of energy or feel that it's enough.

o   Tear into pieces thick stack of old papers or magazine. It should be difficult but possible to tear them.

o   Punching a pillow.

o   Exercising (should be appropriate for your fitness level).

o   Boxing with a punching bag.

Exercise. Make a list of actions that you can take to release your anger in a safe way. Then try some of them.

1._____

2._____

3._____

4._____

5._____

6._____

<u>Nourishing activities in everyday life.</u> Nourishing activities are something that brings you satisfaction and pleasure, reduces stress, and enhances your wellbeing. You need consciously plan nourishing activities in your daily life because they are usually the first thing we sacrifice if we are busy. I split nourishing activities into two categories: big activities and small activities.

Big nourishing activity is something that requires planning, for example, making an appointment for massage therapy, organizing a meeting with friends, or going for a day hike. Small nourishing activity is something that you can do easily and it doesn't require a lot of time. For example, you can have a fifteen minutes nap, pet your cat, give a hug to your partner, read a book, have a walk, buy coffee and so on.

Exercise. Write down one big nourishing activity for each of the four weeks and actions that you need to take and organize it.

Week 1.

Big nourishing activity_____

Actions_____

Week 2.

Big nourishing activity_____

Actions_____

Week 3.

Big nourishing activity_____

Actions_____

Week 4.

Big nourishing activity_____

Actions_____

Exercise. Write down small nourishing activity for each of the seven days.

1._____

2._____

3._____

4._____

5._____

6._____

7._____

4. Emotional Intelligence

Emotional intelligence means that you are able to recognize, tolerate, and express your emotions. It also includes the ability to understand other people's feelings. These skills are extremely important in understanding yourself: your needs, current condition, necessary actions, and in communication with others.

I had difficulties with recognizing and expressing my emotions because of past traumatic experiences. Working with a counsellor, I was able to heal my emotional wounds. It became easier to disclose my emotions to other people.

The best discovery I made is that I can't be responsible for other people's reactions and for their emotional response. It was a great relief to understand that it is not my responsibility to make anyone happy or satisfied. I don't need to blame myself anymore if somebody or a close person experiences unpleasant feelings. I became more resilient when I returned their responsibility back to them.

CHAPTER 10
HOW TO FIND YOURSELF

In life, we regularly question our identity, trying to understand who we are, who we want to be, what we like, what are our dreams and so on. Sometimes our identity can be too rigid that it prevents us from adjusting to the new reality of our life, causing unsatisfaction and depressed feelings. In another situation, identity can be fragile or narrow, making us unconfident and anxious.

When I was discovering myself and going through life transitions, it was extremely helpful to look at my identity and uniqueness from different angles. Below there are some exercises that I found very valuable.

Exercise "Extend your identity."
Part 1. Answer the question "Who am I?" and write your answers down. Your list can be small or big. Try not to think too much; just put down what comes to your mind. Your answer can be one word long or includes a few words.

_____   _____

_____   _____

_____   _____

_____   _____

_____   _____

_____   _____

_____   _____

_____   _____

_____   _____

_____   _____

_____   _____

_____   _____

_____   _____

_____   _____

Part 2. There are four dimensions of your identity: physical, social, personal, and spiritual.

Physical dimension: your appearance, your physical qualities, gender, race, and also physical items that are in your possession. For example, if I am to describe myself, I would say:

a woman, medium height, bald, flexible, have scars, like to try new activities, my upper back muscles are often tight, have a car, collect souvenir spoons, etc.

Physical Dimension
Move words/phrases from the first part of this exercise that match physical dimension to the table below.

Physical Dimension of My Identity

Social dimension: your social roles, you as a member of various social groups. For example, if I am to describe myself, I would say:

wife, daughter, sister, author, personal trainer, Olympian, skier, Russian, Canadian, public speaker, YouTuber, a resident of Vancouver Island, a member of a networking group, a person who does cross-stitching and birdwatching

Social Dimension
Move words/phrases from the first part of this exercise that match social dimension to the table below.

Social Dimension of My Identity

Personal dimension: your character traits, what you like and dislike, your individuality. For example, if I am to describe myself I would say:

optimistic, resilient, anxious, sensitive, emotional; like psychology, travelling, playing guitar and singing; can't eat spicy food, hate boiled milk, love cottage cheese and rye bread; like to read, learn, ride my bicycle, and be with my family.

Personal Dimension
Move words/phrases from the first part of this exercise that match personal dimension to the table below.

Personal Dimension of My Identity

Spiritual dimension: religion, beliefs, moments when you feel yourself as being part of something big, spiritual practice, and volunteering activities. For example, if I am to describe myself, I would say:

A person who feels connection with the world through nature (when I spend time outdoors in a calm or serene environment), a member of Obesity Canada (a charity organization), and not a religious person.

Spiritual Dimension
Move words/phrases from the first part of this exercise that match spiritual dimension to the table below.

Spiritual Dimension of My Identity

Part 3. Have a look at all four tables (four dimensions). What do you think about your identity? Are there more words/phrases in some tables than in others? Would you like to change something?

o   If there are negative descriptions in some of the tables, transform them into neutral or positive ones. By "negative descriptions," I mean rude or critical words such as, for example, ugly, fat, stupid, or clumsy. For instance, the word "stupid" can be substituted with the phrase "not as clever as I expect myself to be."

It is also beneficial to think about why you see yourself in that way. Often we internalize negative attitudes towards ourselves from significant people. Who told you, for example, that you are stupid? Who expected you to be clever?

o   If there are just a few words in some dimensions, try to add more.

o   Think about what you want and what you don't want to have in your identity in the future. Add a desirable characteristic of identity to a relative dimension (table). Cross out everything that you don't want to have in your identity from the dimensions (tables). How did it make you feel? What actions can you take to realize it?

Sometimes our mind doesn't believe instantly that it is possible to change a part of our identity. I found out that in this case, it is helpful to write down a phrase that represents my transition from one characteristic of my identity to another. For example, if I want to cross out "anxious" from personal dimension and put down "calm," I would substitute "anxious" with "in the process of being calmer" or "am learning how to be more relaxed." This way, it is easier for me to believe that changes are possible because they are perceived as gradual.

Finding yourself also includes understanding what you like and dislike, what you want or don't want, and awareness about your values.

Exercise. Write down things, activities and so on that you like and why (e.g., describe your emotions, bodily sensations, thoughts)

Thing/Activity   Why I do like it

_____   _____

_____   _____

_____   _____

_____   _____

_____   _____

_____   _____

_____   _____

_____   _____

_____   _____

_____   _____

_____   _____

_____   _____

_____   _____

Exercise. Write down things, activities and so on that you do NOT like and why (e.g., describe your emotions, bodily sensations, thoughts).

Thing/Activity   Why I don't like it

_____   _____

_____   _____

_____   _____

_____   _____

_____   _____

_____   _____

_____   _____

_____   _____

_____   _____

_____   _____

_____   _____

_____   _____

_____   _____

Be Bold!

REFERENCES

1. Adler, R.B., Rosenfeld, L.B., Proctor II, R.F., & Winder, C. (2012). *Interplay: the process of interpersonal communication.* Don Mills, Ont.: Oxford University Press

2. Vanlint, N., (2017, December). *The Positive Benefits of Creativity.* Retrieved from https://lifelabs.psychologies.co.uk/users/8838-nicola-vanlint/posts/4292-the-positive-benefits-of-creativity

3. Rosenberg, R. (2017). *Accessing the healing power of the vagus nerve: self-help exercises for anxiety, depression, trauma, and autism.* Berkeley, CA: North Atlantic Books

ABOUT THE AUTHOR

After retirement from professional sport in 2014, Elena Muratova immersed herself in helping people. She started her personal training business in 2015. A few years later, Elena began to offer weight loss/lifestyle coaching. She wanted to help people see excess weight as a complex problem and give them more natural and safe ways for going back to self-love and healthy weight.

Her huge interest in psychology brought Elena back to studying. In addition to constantly taking online courses, she attended Canadian college to study psychology. Elena is also enrolled in long-term educational program in Existential Analysis, the approach to counselling which helps a person to find a way to live fulfilled life and give inner consent to his/her actions.

Since 2018, Elena is also a public speaker. By going out into the world, telling her story and sharing helpful tools, Elena hopes to support and inspire people who might be going through difficult time or feel stuck.

To learn more about Elena and her services, please, visit her website

www.elenamuratova.com

To get more information about Elena's weight loss/lifestyle coaching services please visit

www.happybodycentre.com

Made in the USA
San Bernardino, CA
14 February 2020

64404294R00084